Crafting Messages in a Multimodal Media Environment:
Readings on Convergent Writing

John P. McHale, Ph.D., Editor

Illinois State University

Kendall Hunt
publishing company

Cover image © Shutterstock, Inc.

www.kendallhunt.com
Send all inquiries to:
4050 Westmark Drive
Dubuque, IA 52004-1840

Copyright © 2013 by John P. Hale

ISBN 978-1-4652-3196-3

Printed in the United States of America
10 9 8 7 6 5 4 3 2

In appreciative memory of Hunter S. Thompson (1937–2005)

Pioneer of Gonzo Journalism.

To fighting the evil bastards, fueled with rage.

Find and fight them with ink, type, text,

symbols, signs, and stories.

Assistant Editors

Feddersen, K.

Finch, T.

Firmand, M.

Gee, J.

Goebig, J.

Green, R.

Greenstein, J.

Haynes, S.

Kastor, A.

Pelusi, A.

Pillow, J.

Rahn, A.

Smederovac, M.

Suess, S.

Contents

Contents

Chapter 1

Introduction to Multimodal Media Writing

by

John P. McHale, Ph.D.

"Those who can't do, teach. Those who can't teach, teach gym." This quote is from Woody Allen's 1977 film *Annie Hall*, which won the Academy Award for best picture and was nominated for best original screenplay. While of dubious veracity when applied to all teaching situations, the joke has an element of truth. With the value of actual experience in mind, I have tried, in this book, to collect chapters on multimodal media writing from those with practical experience in their respective fields. This edition presents the distillation of decades of valuable experience from respective writing fields. An undercurrent of much of this is the media writer must establish, develop, and maintain healthy working relationships with supervisors, co-workers, clients, sources of information, people who are the subjects of stories, target publics, and audiences.

This supplemental edition of collected essays is designed to help students studying writing for multimodal media. In this introduction, I will preview the salient ideas in each chapter, to thank those who facilitated the completion of this edition, and to summarize the essential idea articulated throughout: multimodal media writing requires a good story, quality writing, and consideration of structural considerations. Most importantly, aspiring writers must dedicate themselves to a life-long journey to become the best writers they can be.

Contributing authors were asked to provide a 1,000- to 1,500-word essay detailing aspects of their area of expertise that they thought beginning multimodal media writing students should be aware. This edition is also designed as an addendum to the textbook *Mass Media Writing: Telling a Good Story Well* by Dr. John P. McHale (Kendall Hunt Publishing). That text emphasizes the importance of telling an intriguing humanized story, structural considerations (unity, pace, variety, and climax), and stresses the importance of quality multimodal media writing (clear, concise, correct, and complete). Contributors were encouraged to emphasize these

1

elements in their contribution. In addition, the development of a convergence media landscape, and the ability for students to write across platforms, can be very important in the employment market. Contributors' experiences offer valuable insight for writing students.

Dr. Megan Hopper explains how a writer can most effectively approach straight news writing (for print or posting on the internet). Hopper outlines the challenge of crafting an effective inverted pyramid story. Hopper explains why the inverted pyramid was developed, and why it is particularly useful for specific purposes. Hopper concludes that inverted pyramid remains a valuable news format despite the rapidly changing multimodal media environment.

Dr. Phillip Chidester provides a superlative discussion of crafting a feature story as opposed to a straight news piece. The key, according to Chidester, is that the writer presents a compelling story, a dramatic narrative that draws a reader in at the cognitive and emotional levels. Chidester delineates the differences between writing straight news and features news. First, features are true stories, with dramatic elements. Second, news pieces have a topic while features have a theme. Third, news pieces have people while features have characters. Fourth, news pieces provide information but features provide description. Fifth, news pieces have one style while features have a range of styles. Chidester concludes that it is important for aspiring feature writers to dedicate themselves to working on developing their own unique storytelling style and voice.

Dave Kindred explains that in a period typified by rapid development and adoption of new communication technologies, a good story well told is still the gold standard. Kindred, an award-winning sportswriter for 45 years, has written for such publications as the *Washington Post* and published nine books. Kindred compares the role of the sports writer, and news writers in general, before the development and adoption of digital media technologies. Kindred's piece contains excellent stories about the exciting and challenging career of a reporter, particularly the sports reporter. Regardless of the modality, reporting is hard work, done in a hurry. Sports writing has taken more than an evolutionary step, complicated by a challenging economic climate. Nevertheless, fundamentals remain crucial. The aspiring media writer must learn to recognize a story and learn to tell it with a beginning, middle, and end. The media writer must also master today's tools. A good story well told is the writer's highest goal. Today, there are more ways to tell a story.

Laura Trendle-Polus, in her chapter, "Writing for Television News," suggests the writer should afford high consideration to the features of the intended audience. It is also important to carefully tailor your intended message to that particular audience. Finally, writing well is as important in writing television news as it is in all other media forms. What that means in a given television news station may vary, so it is wise, when in doubt, to ask *your boss*. Finally, always consider the dramatic values of a television news story.

In the chapter "Copywriting for Television," Dr. Brent K. Simonds identifies career fields for the writer of television spots (commercials, promos, or public service announcements), including advertising agencies, production companies, and television stations (creative services, promotions, or marketing). Writers should use particular strategies in commercial airtime to increase sales of goods and services, directly or indirectly. Simonds also reiterates the importance of developing relationships with those who hire writers of television advertising.

Peter Smudde and Jeffrey Courtright offer a comprehensive consideration of the relationship between tactics and strategy in public relations writing. Smudde and Courtright highlight the need to recognize the importance of the larger strategic picture when crafting individual tactical communication pieces in public relations. Smudde and Courtright discuss the demands of the public relations writing process. They also reiterate the necessity for public relations writing to incorporate traditional features of quality writing. Smudde and Courtright identify that in a convergent media environment, the medium and the message must be considered in tandem. The public relations writer must consider the dynamic interaction between the message and the medium. In essence, particular mediums require modification of potential messages. Smudde and Courtright conclude by highlighting that aspiring public relations writers must recognize they are merely taking the first steps in a lifetime voyage of becoming the best public relations writer they can become.

Alex Hedlund's piece on pitching dramatic programming offers the unique insight of a professional Hollywood reader, those who wallow through stacks of scripts and treatments to find the gems that deserve the attention of those who can make a decision to green light a project. Hedlund offers sound insight into the pitch process for a feature film or a television program. Hedlund presents advice for those who wish to pitch a dramatic program (selling an idea to an insider who can make a writer's idea into an actual film or television show). He outlines the necessary components of a treatment: a logline, a synopsis, and a longer narrative description of the entire film or program. Hedlund's contribution is full of 'dos and don'ts' for the aspiring dramatic writer.

Zach Parcell identifies that the radio industry is constantly changing, evolving into a full blown multimedia power. The addition of online web streaming and mobile applications has expanded radio audiences. This presents new challenges to radio writers who must expand their skill set. Parcell challenges aspiring multimodal radio writers to ask themselves several questions as they grow into proficient and marketable message creators. *What do I write about? What is the appropriate length for online posts? Do writers need to follow AP style in new formats? How formal should writing be in new modalities? Where can writers find content? How can the radio writer use social media?* Parcell concludes by suggesting that, whatever the means of communication, content is important and writers should have fun as they adopt in new modalities.

Kristi Zimmerman discusses the concerns of those crafting social media for corporate communication with potential audiences. Zimmerman focuses upon consideration of audiences and identifies how social media developments allow corporations to more effectively target intended audience members. This allows writers to more effectively tailor messages to segmented audiences. Zimmerman suggests use of nomenclature appropriate for more segmented audiences is more effective than for traditionally more diverse audiences in older mass media forms. Social media also has more opportunities for audience feedback than traditional media forms. She highlights the particular structural considerations for new social media, and identifies the importance of quality writing within social media contexts. Zimmerman concludes that writers must dedicate themselves to continually reevaluating and refining social media communication.

Many people helped make this book possible. Graduate students enrolled in Communication 460: Teaching Mass Media Writing played an important editorial function and worked with contributors to prepare these chapters designed to prepare students to enter the professional world of convergent media writing. These assistant editor graduate students included: K. Feddersen, T. Finch, M. Firmand, J. Gee, J. Goebig, R. Green, J. Greenstein, S. Haynes, A. Kastor, A. Pelusi, J. Pillow, A. Rahn, M. Smederovac, and S. Suess. I am appreciative of their important contributions. I am also grateful for the support of Dr. Larry Long, Director of the Illinois State University School of Communication, and Stephen Hunt, Assistant Director of the Illinois State University School of Communication. Obviously, this edited work would not be possible without the hard work and valuable knowledge of the contributing authors. Their wisdom will help students let their inner light shine in their future multimodal-media writing endeavors.

In sum, stories are important. The contributing authors repeatedly reiterate the importance of strong storytelling and quality writing, regardless of the modality of the media. First, in whatever medium, audiences are drawn to good stories that incorporate basic features of compelling narratives, including a protagonist who acts on a will or wants to achieve a goal despite complications. Second, quality writing is clear, correct, complete, and concise. Third, the writer in any venue should be cognizant of structural considerations including pace, variety, unity, and, of course, climax, in which a dramatic question or comedic setup is resolved. Relationships are important in all these areas of writing. Throughout these chapters, authors from a diverse professional background challenge the aspiring multimodal media writer to dedicate themselves to the life-long pursuit of becoming a better writer. Becoming a better writer is a fulfilling journey without a final destination.

Chapter 2

The Inverted Pyramid Style: A Brief History

by

K. Megan Hopper

A nearly 400-pound Bengal tiger escaped the trailer its owner was hauling it across the country in today at a local truck stop. The tiger roamed around unsupervised in a well-populated residential area close to the truck stop before hunkering down in a small patch of trees, making sure to put everyone nearby on edge with a few periodic roars. You, a beginning reporter at the local daily newspaper, are assigned to cover the story and have been sitting at the truck stop for most of the day watching and waiting to see how the owner, law enforcement, and animal control officials will deal with the situation. You interview the owner, who is visibly distraught and talks at length about how worried she is about the tiger and how hopeful she is it will be able to return to her unharmed. You then speak to individuals who own homes close to where the tiger now sits. They are most concerned with the tiger being removed from the area in whatever way possible to return their neighborhood to safety. After several failed attempts at tranquilization, the standoff finally comes to an end with animal control having to kill the tiger. After this occurs, you get a chance to interview the officer who shot the fatal blow. He is shaken at having to resort to such measures, but indicates it was all part of his job. What would be the best way to structure the reporting of this story? Which of these facts would you tell first?

In the case of hard, breaking news such as an escaped tiger in the community, most news organizations would use the inverted pyramid style of writing to convey the story to readers. The inverted pyramid style requires a reporter to lead the story with a summary of the most important information first, rather than waiting until the end of the story to provide the most key details.

The escaped tiger was one of the first breaking news stories I covered as a rookie reporter. I followed the inverted pyramid style to write the following lead for *The Pantagraph*, a daily newspaper in Bloomington, Illinois:

BLOOMINGTON—A Bengal tiger weighing approximately 390 pounds was shot and killed Saturday after escaping from a trailer at the Travelcenters of America truck stop in Bloomington.

The second paragraph in an inverted pyramid style is nearly as crucial of an element to the story as the lead, as this paragraph builds on the lead and encourages readers to continue reading. The second paragraph in my tiger story read as follows:

The 2-year-old, 8-foot-long male tiger named Tigger was reported missing at about 5 a.m. Saturday when it got away from its owner at the truck stop at the junction of Interstate 55/74 and Market Street in Bloomington.

In subsequent paragraphs comprising the body of the story, information should be given in descending order of importance. This is where I placed a variety of direct quotes and supporting information gathered from the tiger's owner, nearby homeowners, and officials, as well as any descriptive details about the scene.

The inverted pyramid style of writing requires several judgment calls a reporter must make in regard to where to place the information he/she has gathered. Rich (2010) suggests writing an inverted pyramid style story requires asking yourself what information should be included in the lead that the reader needs to know first, what information is needed to explain any pieces of the story absent from the lead, what information impacts the reader the most, and what order should quotes and supporting information follow. Although the most important information, or climax, of the story appears at the beginning, a reporter must still attempt to craft a unified and interesting body and ending. Unity can be achieved through the use of effective transitional phrases that guide the reader clearly down the pyramid as the pace of the story starts to slow down.

The history of the inverted pyramid style of news writing can be traced back to the 1860s and journalistic techniques that developed during reporting of the Civil War. This style of writing was partly born out of the difficulties those reporting on the war faced when trying to send accounts of actions on the battlefields back to their respective newsrooms. The telegraph, although a speedy way to transmit messages, was costly to news organizations and was often unreliable as the lines regularly broke causing newsroom reception of stories from the field to be broken off often before the most important information had been transmitted. Many editors then decided to call for changes in the ways news reporters structured their stories. From that point on, reporters were instructed to place key information first in a story and then work their way down placing gathered information in decreasing order of importance (Kershner, 2012). Thus, the inverted pyramid style of writing was conceived out of a need to ensure that even if a telegraph, or any other type of transmission of the story, were interrupted the most important information would still be told.

Engaging in reporting and writing for the mass media should be done with this key period in history in mind. Beginning reporters should pretend as if the reception of their straight print news story could potentially be broken up at any point in time. Whether that interruption is due to technological failings, or simply due to a reader losing interest, any good reporter must write accordingly. A skilled reporter makes sure to clearly and concisely phrase the information that his or her story absolutely could not afford to lose at the top of the story, mostly within the lead paragraph. Even if the transmission of your story is lost after the first paragraph, the reader should still know the main point of your story including the most important facts such as who, what, where, when, why and how.

Writing an inverted pyramid style story can often be difficult for beginning reporters, as this style of writing is contradictory to the narrative style with which we have learned to tell stories to others. Usually, storytellers prefer to build up to the climax of their stories providing background detail and supporting facts in the beginning and middle and then ending with the most important information and some sort of resolution or outcome. When telling stories in everyday life, we like to grab the audience's attention, interest the audience in some way, maintain that attention and interest, and have them continually wondering "And then what?" until they finally reach the end of the story.

Inverted pyramid style follows an opposite structure whereby you cover the good stuff first, you tell the end of the story in the beginning. This is a hard style of writing to adjust to as we are often annoyed when novels, television shows, movies, etc. of interest are "spoiled" by someone giving away the ending before we have had the chance to read/see the entire details of the story for ourselves. However, reporters need to remind themselves that this style of writing is essential in ensuring that readers obtain necessary information quickly. It allows for readers to not waste their time figuring out whether or not they are interested in a story and it allows for editors to easily determine portions of the story that can be cut prior to publication by working from the bottom up when space is an issue.

Despite lacking some of the creative possibilities that the narrative style of storytelling and feature writing allow for, inverted pyramid stories still require good writing. Reporters still need to explain how the story affects readers and need to do so in a clear, concise, and interesting manner. Further, opportunities for creative writing in an inverted pyramid story are still present, especially in the detail the reporter adds by careful selection of the best quotes and through accurate yet colorful description of the scene.

Although it has been around for more than 150 years, the inverted pyramid style for straight news continues to work well when writing for the web in a rapidly converging media environment. On a multimedia platform, space may not always be as big of a concern as on a traditional print platform, but providing the most important information in a quick and concise fashion remains a crucial factor in both cases. Mark Pickering, editor of *The Pantagraph,* a daily newspaper in Bloomington, Illinois, believes inverted pyramid is an even more crucial style of writing breaking news for news websites. At *The Pantagraph,* reporters post breaking news as it happens with three or four sentences informing online readers of the most recent and most important information. They then "layer" the story as it develops, adding details as the reporter gathers them. According to Pickering, "In these cases, the inverted pyramid style not only is the most effective way to report the story, I think, but really is the only way for an editor to ensure the story is complete and posted ASAP."

Benjamin Davis (2010), an accomplished journalist and new media news lecturer, suggests in a post on the *Online Journalism Review* the inverted pyramid style, although still valid, needs updating when crafting news stories for a digital internet audience. He advocates the use of a "digital media pyramid" that by no means takes the place of the inverted pyramid. Rather, the digital media pyramid improves upon the traditional style of writing straight print news to better suit the highly converged media atmosphere we are currently immersed in. This updated style of writing still involves placing the most important of the who, what, where, when, why, and how of a story in the lead paragraph. However, in the digital media pyramid, the lead is set apart from the rest of the story even further by reporters presenting it in bold text and often linking the text of the lead to another page where the rest of the story is located.

As for the body of the story, Davis (2010) states the digital media pyramid structure urges reporters to properly search for, cut and paste, and properly attribute supporting information for the story available from other internet sources all while complying with copyright laws. In a further consideration of the opportunities afforded by the web, the digital media pyramid stresses the importance of strategic use of photographs, video, interactivity, and all other nontextual elements not addressed by the traditional inverted pyramid. Those writing for the web also need to consider how the placement of certain advertisements next to or inside their stories might communicate potential bias or unintended meaning.

Last, the digital media pyramid allows for reporters to push their readers to go beyond the contents of the story and to look for opposing and/or diverse views on a subject. By inserting links to other websites that contain this information as well as any other relevant resources, reporters can still avoid the lengthy stories that the traditional inverted pyramid was initially created to cease, yet also provide their readers with the tools to further inform themselves in a balanced fashion.

Regardless of the platform you are writing for, clear, concise, interesting, and credible writing remain key skills in the journalism field today. The inverted pyramid style aids a reporter in crafting a well-told story while also allowing the reporter to communicate the most important information quickly and succinctly. As the obstacle of having busy and often impatient readers have replaced complications such as unreliable telegraph transmissions, the need to get to the point of a story as soon as possible is as crucial as ever.

Edited by Traci Finch

About K. Megan Hopper

Before receiving her B.S. in mass communication and M.S. in communication from Illinois State University and her Ph.D. in communication from the University of Missouri, Dr. Hopper served as a reporter for *The Pantagraph* and *The Daily Vidette*. While with the *Vidette*, she received the Best Beat Reporter award in 2002, among others. Hopper is a member of the National Communication Association, the Central States Communication Association, and the Cultural Studies Association.

References

Davis, B. (2010). The need for a 'digital media pyramid.' *Online Journalism Review*. Retrieved from http://www.ojr.org/ojr/people/bendavis/201002/1823/.

Kershner, J.W. (2012). *The elements of news writing* (3rd ed.). Boston, MA: Allyn & Bacon.

Rich, C. (2010). *Writing and reporting news: A coaching method* (6th ed.). Boston, MA: Wadsworth, Cengage Learning.

Chapter 3

Telling a Feature Story: What Happened?

by

Phil Chidester, Ph.D.

There, in that moment, I might have focused my attention on just about anything: the bits of filthy gravel digging themselves into the tender skin of my cheek, just above the jawbone; the press of cold pavement against my ribcage as my heart kept time with the thrumming of passing cars; the faint echoes of voices, a kind of distant horror as worried feet pounded closer and closer.

I might have paid attention to just about anything—but instead I kept staring at the wheel of the ten-speed as it spun slowly to a stop next to my head, the spokes clickety-clacking every time they passed that pedal, a form once so steely perfect, now misshapen somehow, twisted self-consciously in on itself from the impact.

What does it mean to tell a story? Or maybe more accurately, *why* do we tell stories in the first place? And understanding *why* we tell stories, *how* can we work, day by day, to improve our abilities as journalists to not only tell them, but to tell them well?

Perhaps the most important thing that any of us who teach writing could ever say about the craft of producing effective features is that we should always remember this one crucial fact: features are *stories*. Stories through and through, opening, exposition and close, "once upon a time" right through to "and they lived happily ever after." And not just any kind of story either. A great feature is the kind of story that fills every inch of the space that's been set aside for it with real life and color; the kind of story that keeps its audience riveted to a spot, almost afraid to breathe for fear of whispering away the magic; the kind of story that cannot wait to be told and retold, again and again.

Most of all, a great feature is the kind of story that is going to test your mettle as a storyteller, and at every stage of the long, challenging writing process too—from the moment when the germ of an idea is planted in your imagination right through to the last line of the final draft.

So what does it take to write a great feature?

At first glance, the answer is obvious: great features come from great experiences. Let's face it—some events or happenings in life are so forceful, so compelling, so incredibly memorable that they pretty much tell themselves. Just imagine being one of the newspaper folks assigned to cover the maiden voyage of the *Titanic* around the turn of the last century. Pride and arrogance, fabulous wealth and humble poverty, courage and faintheartedness, tragedy and loss: all the material you could ever dream of was there for the plucking, ready to be collected and shaped into the kind of story that people a century later would still be talking about.

Maybe it is true every once in a while; maybe some stories are just so good that it really doesn't matter who tells them, or even how they are told. Maybe readers are so caught up in the details of the best stories that they're virtually fool-proof. Maybe it is true—but I am thinking I have seen too many terrible remakes of some pretty amazing classic Hollywood movies to believe that for a minute.

Because if the story really is an important part of the process (I cannot imagine anyone, no matter how talented a writer, coming up with a gripping tale about the items on a Saturday afternoon grocery shopping list), the storyteller is as important a player in the creation of the perfect feature. Maybe even more important: Don't we all know at least one friend, acquaintance, family member who could not "story" his or her way out of a folded paper bag? There is nothing more painful than listening to a storytelling hack positively butcher what should have been a really ripping yarn, is there? It is pure torture—sitting idly by, fighting that urge to slip in and edit a little here and there, to add a detail, to polish up the timing just a touch, to save the rest of the guests at the dinner party the misery of listening one moment more. What agony to know that this special story could be told so much better, that it *deserves* so much better, and we're not the ones telling it!

(Just a note: If you're sensing any guilt at all for having these kinds of feelings about the hack storytellers we all run into from time to time, please don't. After all, the plumber doesn't [or at least shouldn't] feel the least bit awkward about coming over to fix the toilet in my house that I'm so incapable of repairing myself. If we truly are the storytellers of today, if it truly is our calling to share this gift with the world, then we need to be confident about our abilities to do so, and to do so better than most of the people who will experience and enjoy what we write for them.)

In summary, writing effective features is one part discovering the best stories to tell, one part bringing our best storytelling skills to the table. Just one problem: Far too often the training we receive as journalists seems to rip out—or at the very least, to numb—our very best storytelling instincts. Course after course about AP Style considerations and inverted pyramids and delayed identification leads and, perhaps worst of all, "unbiased and objective reporting" have left far too many of us rethinking our roles as storytellers. In the ongoing quest to share "just the facts, ma'am" with our readers, we've forgotten the craft of storytelling. Many have concluded, instead, that our job is to collect the details at one end of the communication chain and to simply relay them at the other. Many have become, in the end, nothing more than the waxed string that connects the two Campbell's soup cans in the classic childhood telephone experiment. Ours is not to question, or to consider, or even to filter; ours is to simply pass along, then move on to the next story.

This is not to suggest that there are not many situations in which our aim as journalists is to do precisely that—to get the information as quickly and as efficiently and as accurately as possible into the hands of our readers. They call the people who fill this "waxed string" role news reporters—and every good journalist should be able to take on this responsibility in an ethical, professional, and proficient way whenever such efforts are expected and required. But every good journalist must also be ready to serve as an ethical, professional, and consistently excellent *storyteller* whenever the opportunity presents itself as well. And to be a bona fide storyteller means to do much more than to transmit information from a source to an audience. True storytellers transform the material that comes into their hands; they focus it, they elevate it to something much greater than its constituent parts, and then they share with their audiences a reading experience that is as much art as it is information.

One of the many keys to effective journalism practice, then, is to recognize the times when these two very different roles of the journalist are demanded by the situation, and also expected by the reader. And perhaps the easiest way to keep the two roles straight is to point out that news stories are produced by journalists-as-reporters, while features are created by journalists-as-storytellers. The danger in drawing such broad distinctions, of course, is creating the impression that the two roles are entirely different for the journalist in the trenches—and nothing could be further from the truth. Both reporters and storytellers deal in facts, and both need to be impeccable in the collection and transmitting of those facts to their readers. Both also turn to the interview as the lifeblood of their profession; in other words, readers of both news and features expect their writers/storytellers to make contact with the most important people at the heart of the stories they tell, and to pass along what they discover through these encounters. But beyond these key similarities, reporters and storytellers really do fill very different roles as they pursue their distinct crafts. And perhaps the best way of understanding the vital function of journalist-storyteller, particularly in our media-saturated world of today, is to take a quick peek at the fundamental differences between the products generated by the reporter and the storyteller as they work to share their impressions of the world with their many readers.

What most clearly distinguishes the feature from the news story? The easy answer is length. Feature stories are nearly always longer than news, and not just a little longer either; sometimes they're three to four times longer than the typical news piece. But length alone certainly cannot account for the different functions that are served by the two types of stories. The question is, then, what the feature accomplishes with all that extra verbiage, with all the extra space that such a long story commands on a print page, on an internet website, or in a nightly TV newscast. And it's not just a matter of what we might decide as storytellers to do with the delicious luxury of that extra time and space either. What do audiences expect us to do with all that content? What, exactly, are we going to provide that will keep them focused on a story that is, after all, long enough for three or even four traditional news pieces?

Here, for your consideration, are a few possibilities.

1. Features are true *stories*.

Maybe we in the journalism business call news pieces "stories" out of sheer habit, but that's no excuse for our reporter forebears. Let's face it: news pieces might be wonderful things, but stories they ain't. How many stories do you know that supply all the most important details of the action up front, then gradually sputter to a halt as they move along (inverted pyramid style, anyone?)? It's like telling the punch line of your favorite joke first, then explaining why it's so darned funny. I loved the movie *The Sixth Sense.* Still, I can't even imagine enjoying the film if, in the first few frames, director M. Night Shyamalan had stared into the camera and said, "A young boy with the ability to talk to the dead has helped a child psychiatrist to recognize and embrace the fact that he was shot and killed a few months ago by a distraught patient." I don't know about you, but I kind of enjoyed figuring out that twist for myself, a little at a time, as *The Sixth Sense's* engaging story moved along. The first approach works really well for readers who are interested only in grasping the facts of a particular event quickly and efficiently. But for readers who are expecting a true reading experience, a real *story,* the inverted pyramid simply isn't going to cut it.

Feature readers want an inviting opening, not a traditional news lead; they want satisfying closure on the tale, not a minor detail waiting to be lopped off by a copy editor looking to trim the fat from a bloated news piece. And most of all, feature readers want to get wrapped up in the story they're reading. If they simply wanted information, they'd have no trouble finding it elsewhere. Gone are the days when the daily print newspaper was the audience's sole source of facts about community, state, nation, and world; today the internet is brimming with sites eager to provide exactly that. So as feature writers, we need to figure out how to capture our readers early on, to take them by the hand, to pull them into our tales and set them up for the ride of their lives. Yes, we need to give them good information in the process too, but no reader ever walked away from a truly great feature story thinking, "Just look at everything I've learned today!" Rather, the reaction that marks the truly exceptional feature is one of "What a great story!"—followed, of course, by a slowly dawning recognition of the insights that have come along with a ripping good yarn.

2. News pieces have a *topic*; feature stories have a *theme*.

What makes for a solid news piece? In the journalism business, we spend a lot of time talking about news values or news judgment; we like to point out that any event or happening that meets the audience's expectations for timeliness, proximity, impact, prominence, conflict (drama) and/or novelty (singularity) will likely be received well by the reader. So the subject matter of a news piece is pretty much wide open; it can be literally anything that appeals to your audience. But no matter what the news piece is about content-wise, the approach for the news reporter is always the same. The topic of every news piece you will ever read is this: What Happened. Strip away all the decorative details, the names of the people involved, and the statistics on how strong or how costly or how often, not to mention the quotes from a few participants, and that's what remains. That is why we write news pieces in the first place. Something happened, and it's our job to tell the reader all about it. As a matter of fact, readers' expectations for news pieces are so ingrained that if we try to do anything else in these kinds of accounts besides talking about What Happened, we're pretty sure to irritate at least some of our audience members.

One example: Many traditional publications have moved to the internet, and a number of them invite their reporters to post personal blogs. These blogs operate very much like opinion pieces in the more traditional print format—they give reporters a chance to express their ideas about and attitudes toward the issues they cover. It's funny, though: Many readers do not seem to realize that these are supposed to be opinion pieces, and they vent their frustration in their responses to the blogs. They may not frame things in exactly this way, but it is pretty clear where they're coming from. Reporters aren't supposed to tell me what they think about stuff; they're just supposed to talk about What Happened.

But when it comes to features, What Happened is just the start. Don't get me wrong; What Happened is still a very important component in the great feature. In fact, without any What Happened at all, readers will wonder why the journalist has decided to tell this particular story at this particular time. But once What Happened is out of the way, the storyteller is free to develop a real theme as the story proceeds. Why did What Happened really happen? How has What Happened affected the people involved, especially the people who count themselves among the journalist's reading audience? Who are some of the intriguing personalities at the heart of What Happened? What was it like to be in the middle of What Happened, or to participate in other happenings like this one? Asking and answering in a complete and consistent way these kinds of questions allows the feature to do much more than simply report the facts surrounding a particular event or experience.

It is hard to overestimate the importance of a strong theme to the overall success of a great feature. In fact, if you find that your feature is spending a lot of time discussing What Happened, you've probably produced an overly long, overly detailed news piece, not a feature.

3. News pieces have *people*; features have *characters*.

What's the difference between a person and a character? Look around; the world is full of people. They pop in and out of our lives at unexpected intervals, and once they've moved on, we don't tend to think about them much anymore. The woman who took your scholarship application in the Student Aid Office on Friday morning, the plumber who dropped by to look at my broken toilet yesterday afternoon, that guy your friend introduced you to at the party last weekend—these are people. Don't get me wrong; people can be very useful to us as journalists. People who are experts in certain subjects have important insights to share from time to time, and people who somehow find themselves involved in What Happened are certainly going to draw our attention for a minute or two. But once these moments in the spotlight are over, there's no reason for us to keep thinking about them—they're bit players in the overall daily dramas of our lives.

News pieces are full of people. Depending upon the topic we're writing about, these people might be fire chiefs or police officers, club members or accident witnesses, political science professors or even "typical" students with something to say about the event or happening we're writing about. It's our job to introduce these people to the reader by providing the expected details—full names and job positions, hometowns, majors in school, etc.—and then, often as not, to supply a bit of dialogue in the people's own words. And that is it. In a news piece, it is pretty uncommon to even return to one of these people once he or she has crossed the reader's viewing screen. An introduction, a quick quote, and then it is over. Just like the dozens of people we are introduced to at a weekend party, there's no good reason to concern ourselves with these bit players any further. They have served their useful purpose: time to shake that next hand, to listen to the name and hometown and major of the next party-goer who we'll forget the minute he or she has moved beyond our field of vision.

Feature stories are full of people too—only their function in these kinds of stories is often a little different. Sure, many of them still do shed light on or lend credibility to the What Happened at the heart of the story. But in a number of instances, the role of people in a feature is to help us get to know the *characters* who are the real lifeblood of the feature.

What's the difference between a person and a character? For one, while people are introduced to us as readers, characters are *revealed* to us. In a news piece, the reporter may tell me all I really need to know about a person in a single sentence. In a feature, I may still be learning new things about a character through the final paragraph of the story. If people are the figures we meet and immediately forget at a party, then characters are the ones we develop relationships with. Characters stick around on our personal stages for a while. We identify with them, we care about what happens to them, and we may even relate to their experiences. Characters encourage us to think about how we'd respond if we were in their shoes. And perhaps most importantly, as we see them change as the events in a particular story proceed, characters help us to recognize just how much our own ways of thinking and acting change as we move through life.

So how does the gifted storyteller turn a person into a character in a story? Think about how we come to know the folks who are the most important to us in life. We spend time with them—not just in their public lives, but when they're away from the spotlight, too. We pay attention not only to what they say, but to what they do. We notice the details of their unique surroundings—the cars they drive, the clothes they wear, the things they use to decorate their living spaces. And we listen to what others have to say about them, just in case our own perspectives might be off a little. So if this is how we get to know the important people in our own lives, what's stopping us as storytellers from using these same techniques to reveal important characters to readers in our stories?

I cannot think of a single great feature story that didn't use these details to create at least one memorable character. Of course, nothing says the character has to be a human being; I have read some great stories that have developed characters out of cherished pets, old buildings, even entire towns. But a character who comes to live, breathe—and perhaps most importantly, *evolve*—for the reader is absolutely essential to the effective feature story. Because while a great storyline might draw readers in, it's the characters who they will remember as they walk away from the reading experiences; it is the characters they'll thank you for introducing them to as a great storyteller.

4. News pieces provide *information*; features provide *description*.

As we discussed earlier, the main function of a news piece is to supply information about What Happened. Because news pieces are so brief, every detail included in the text is focused on this one overriding goal; every bit of data has this singular aim. It's pretty easy to tell when a news piece has "gone off the rails." It is when the reporter starts adding details that don't contribute directly to an explanation of What Happened (or, in the case of a preview piece, to What Will Happen). Let's say a local student is hit by a car and seriously injured while crossing a campus street. It wouldn't make sense to spend a paragraph talking about the history of the company that manufactured the car that was involved in the accident, or about company employees' charitable efforts either. These details don't have anything at all to do with What Happened, so they simply don't belong in the news piece.

Not to suggest that good news reporters would even think of going off on tangents like that. In fact, as journalists, we're constantly reminded to keep our work free of just these kinds of extra details. But as that message is consistently and persistently drummed into our heads, I am afraid we tend to walk away with the impression that all details are bad, that they take away from the central facts of an event or happening—and perhaps worst of all, that they tend to reveal our personal biases as reporters. In the quest to be ever objective, we as journalist-reporters often abandon one of the most important tools in our arsenal, a tool that is absolutely fundamental to creating effective stories as journalist-storytellers.

What role does description play in the great feature? For one, supplying readers with the sensory details that accompany a given event or experience is a great way of putting audiences "in the moment." If the most powerful stories are those that help readers to feel as if they have experienced its events for themselves, then description is the engine that drives this sharing, this communion. If I as a reader can truly put myself in the main character's shoes, then I am going to walk away from the reading of a story having experienced something very memorable indeed. What's it like to win the Super Bowl as a quarterback? To work as a server in a local dive bar? To jump out of an airplane? It's one thing to ask a person who isn't a professional storyteller to describe the sensations for you and then quote this person directly—but why would you trust a non-storyteller with such an important task? It's another thing entirely to use your heightened skills as a journalist-storyteller to focus on pertinent details and describe them yourself for the reader.

Beyond immersing readers in the sights, sounds, smells, tastes, and feelings of a given moment, description also helps audiences get to know your main characters. If journalism is a game of kindergarten show and tell, then it's pretty obvious. News pieces *tell*; feature stories *show*. If you're writing a news piece, you probably don't have the space or time to do much more than *tell* the reader that the parents of the missing child were nervous during their interview with the media in front of their home. But if you're putting together a feature intended to immerse the reader in the experience of dealing with this kind of loss, then you've got some time and space to play with—so why not *show* readers the nervousness? Give them the beads of moisture on their foreheads, glistening in the hot TV spotlights; give them the sound of sniffling as the wife barely holds back her tears; give them that unmistakable scent of stale sweat and fear.

And description can do so much more than put readers in a moment or help them relate to your characters, too. Think about it: everyone who approaches your story will do so from one of two broad perspectives. No matter what person or event or experience you're focusing on in your story, some readers will be familiar with it, and others will not. So how do you appeal to both kinds of readers as you write? For readers who have not experienced what you are writing about, the challenge is to convince them as they walk away from your story that they now have had this experience for themselves—and including effective description is going to be your key to achieving this goal. And for those who have already experienced what your story's talking about? The key in this case is to give them a whole new perspective on a familiar theme or experience. Once again, effective description is going to go a long way in helping you to do this.

What do I mean by "effective description"? Details can't be simply added for details' sake; readers will sniff out the tactic in a minute. Don't tell me what a character is wearing on a particular afternoon, for example, if doing so isn't going to help me understand or relate to the character, or if that description isn't going to move the action along. Don't get so bogged down in describing the scene that you forget that something needs to happen in that scene. Far too often, beginning storytellers in particular get so busy describing elements of the scene that the What Happened gets completely lost in the clutter. Remember that description has a purpose; to put readers in the moment, to reveal character, to help readers relate. And finally, be extra careful with adjectives. A few here and there are fine, but if you read back through your paragraphs and discover that everything in the world of your story is thick, or sunny, or warm, or sparkly, then you're likely obscuring something important with the fluff. Keep in mind, too, that adjectives more often than not can tend to reveal your opinion as the storyteller. There is a world of difference between "Tickets are $5" and "Tickets are *only* $5," isn't there?

5. News pieces have *one style*; features have a *range of styles*.

Readers expect us to approach things in a certain way when we put together our news pieces as journalist-reporters. The *AP Style Guide* does a great job of helping us figure out exactly what those expectations look like. Which numbers do we list as numerals, and which ones do we spell out as words? What's the correct abbreviation for "California"? How do you properly cite the job titles for church reverends or university presidents? Should we capitalize departments? Is it okay to use abbreviations? Taken together, all these rules help us to be consistent as we put together our news pieces—and that's important, both for journalists and for our readers, too.

But style is a whole lot more than abbreviating and capitalizing; it's also about the overall flow of our writing. Ever notice how, no matter what the topic is, every broadcast news piece tends to sound pretty much the same? There is a certain rhythm to the thing, a certain tone of voice, a way of telling the story that suggests a kind of distance from the material, a matter-of-fact perspective on the part of the news anchors. And the same goes for our print news pieces. If we were to read them aloud, they'd all come across in a pretty similar way. It's a style that audiences have become used to after reading literally hundreds of similar-sounding news pieces. For one thing, readers expect us to take the news events we cover pretty seriously. They want us to treat each and every fact as if it were the most important in the story, and thus worthy of our best efforts. Perhaps most of all, they don't want us as journalist-reporters to be walking all over the facts in our large, muddy boots. As far as they're concerned, there's no need for us to even put our names on news pieces. After all, no matter who wrote them, they'd all end up sounding the same. And that is how readers like their news pieces: formal, distant, factual. The expert journalist-reporter would hardly ever dream of addressing the reader directly in a news piece—doing so would force audiences to pay attention to the journalist instead of the story, and that's simply not to be done in this kind of writing. And heaven help the reporter who dares use the word "I" in a news piece; readers would rather stumble through an awkward quote or digest a clearly incorrect fact than even think about the person behind those words on the news page.

Here we find one of the most significant differences between journalist-reporters and journalist-storytellers—because when you're writing a feature, those muddy journalist boots are going to be all over the story you're telling. And believe it or not, readers really prefer things that way. Because it's your personal style, your own unique way of recounting events, that truly turns the journalist into a storyteller, that invites the reader to reconsider familiar experiences or to understand for the first time unfamiliar ones. There's no doubt that the style you use to tell a particular story should depend on the theme of that story. No one's going to be interested in reading a snarky story about child abuse, or a highly critical story about the local carnival. But beyond this basic restriction, the opportunity to write a feature, any feature, is really an opportunity to shape and perfect your voice as a storyteller.

And what is that voice? Is yours a tendency to turn a cynical eye on the events of the world, or are you a melancholy soul? Do you prefer the tongue-in-cheek approach, or do you like to lend a childlike sense of wonder to the subjects in your stories? And beyond these questions, just what is the relationship you encourage your readers to develop with you as a storyteller? Would you like them to sit quietly and listen to the telling? In this case, formal word choices and a calm, gradual rhythm to your sentences is the key. Or maybe you'd prefer to get in readers' faces, to confront them directly with the details of your story, to pull them in by making them a part of the telling. If so, you're going to use less formal language; you are going to use a short, quick sentence structure; and above all else, you're going to use lots of "I" and "you"— to give the appearance of an actual conversation going on.

Whatever style you choose to develop, it is imperative that you keep working to find and polish that unique voice as a storyteller. Because in the final accounting of things, in this media-saturated world we are experiencing today, there is nothing but competition out there for your readers' attentions. What can you bring to the table to keep them focused on your writing? What are you going to provide them that others simply cannot?

I have no doubt that the world will always make a place for good storytellers. It was true for the oldest civilizations on record, and it will be true hundreds of years from now, long after newspapers and TVs and even the internet have been forgotten. Will you be among those who earn a cherished place in society by being one of those outstanding storytellers?

When I began writing this chapter, I struggled for a long time to figure out just how to proceed. I knew I had a lot of important information to share with you. But I didn't know if I wanted to present it in a very formal, textbook kind of way, or if I'd rather take a bit more playful tone. I'm pretty glad now that I decided to include you in the conversation—the same way that many of you might to decide to include your readers in your features from now on.

Thanks for reading. Oh, and in case any of you were wondering about the opening paragraphs, I did get hit by a car on my bike when I was a kid.

Want me to tell you about it?

Edited by Jordan Goebig

About Dr. Phil Chidester

Dr. Phil Chidester is currently an Associate Professor and Coordinator of the Journalism Program at Illinois State University. Dr. Chidester teaches a number of classes on reporting and feature writing, as well as graduate level courses. He completed his masters and doctorate in Communication Studies at the University of Kansas. Phil served as a reporter and staff writer at a daily regional newspaper in Utah, and worked as a lecturer of Communication and director of Advancement Relations at Southern Utah University, where he received his bachelors. Dr. Chidester has presented his work at numerous conferences of the National Communication Association, the International Communication Association, the Central States Communication Association and the Conference on Race at Harvard University, and has received top competitive paper awards from both the NCA and the CSCA.

Chapter 4

Even in a Mass Media Revolution, a Good Story Well Told Is Still the Gold Standard

by Dave Kindred

Here's what sportswriting used to be . . .

Hard work, done in a hurry:

Before a baseball game, the beat writer filed a few notes gathered during batting practice and in casual clubhouse chatter. During the game, he wrote a running account of the action, inning by inning. Afterwards, he hurried to the clubhouses for quotes to insert into his running story. Back in his press box seat, he rewrote it all into a new story. All that work, done at speed, was counterproductive to good reporting, let alone keen observation of a game that rewarded such attention. As for writing anything of a quality much higher than a ransom note, the workload made that impossible.

Here's what sportswriting is today . . .

Hard work, done at warp-speed:

"From the time I get to the ballpark, four hours before a game, until I'm done two hours or so after, I'm writing constantly," said Wally Matthews of ESPN New York. He is a veteran newspaperman, long a boxing reporter and columnist who in 2010 became a baseball beat reporter for the first time. Everything he heard in the clubhouse and dugout was fodder for immediate Twitter feeds and live-blogging. He tape-recorded everything, transcribed the interviews, and re-read the transcripts so if he happened to miss a "news" item while thumbing into his hand-held device, he could drop that essential nugget into his next tweet. He said, "I tell my wife, after 3:30, don't call me unless it's an emergency because I don't have time to talk."

The hustle began, for Matthews and all beat reporters covering the Yankees, when the team's third base coach, Rob Thomson, walked from the clubhouse toward the dugout. He carried that night's lineup card. Routine stuff, that card. It's always posted on the team's dugout wall and has been since Connie Mack was Cornelius

McGillicuddy catching without a mask. Yet the assembled literati snapped to attention when Thomson teased them by waving the card in their faces. They fell in line and followed him to the dugout. That way they were present the second he taped the card up.

"Then," Wally Matthews said, "thumbs start flying."

The reporters thumbed the night's lineup into their hand-held devices because, if they didn't get the lineup into the ether immediately, they heard lamentations from their Twitter followers, their Facebook friends, and that crowd of fanatics who want the lineup now and know they can get it now and won't be happy until the reporters satisfy, if only momentarily, their lust for information.

"Hours before the game," Matthews said, "I'm getting tweets asking, 'Where's the lineup?' It's crazy. The beat guys, it matters if we get the lineup posted first by 45 seconds. We go around saying, 'Look at the time code, I had the lineup way before you.' It's now a world of flying thumbs. It's like those video games I used to get on my 12-year-old son for playing – I'm 53 and now I'm doing it."

Sportswriting has taken more than an evolutionary step. It is in a revolutionary period that is at once inspiring and poignant. A harsh economic climate, exacerbated by the flight of readers and advertisers to the internet, has forced newspapers large and small to reduce their staffs, their expenses, and their ambitions. We are alive to hear the death rattle of an American institution. At the same time, we are present at the birth of a new world of media.

For two years, I worked on a book about *The Washington Post*. The night Barack Obama was elected president, the *Post*'s newsroom was a scene of controlled chaos, adrenaline running high. I heard the newspaper's executive editor, Leonard Downie Jr., say, "News matters"—as if to assure himself his world would last forever.

The work had put me with reporters who risked their lives to tell stories. The foreign correspondent Anthony Shadid told me about being shot by an Israeli soldier at near point-blank range; his colleague, Steve Fainaru, was caught in a firefight the day he arrived in Iraq. I spent months listening to dedicated men and women—among them Dana Priest and Anne Hull, Gene Weingarten, David Broder, David Maraniss—who worried that journalism itself was at risk.

So today's young reporters are at a turning point in journalism's history. For them, if not for wizened reporters left over from newspapers' golden age, these are thrilling times. Those young journalists will thrive if they:

<BL> *Master the fundamentals. Learn to recognize a story, learn to tell it with a beginning, middle, and end.

*Master today's tools. A good story well told remains the gold standard, but the technology has given us a hundred ways to tell our stories more vividly.</BL>

Imagine if I had carried a video camera on July 8, 1974. I interviewed Muhammad Ali as he drove a Cadillac at frightening speed down a narrow, rutted logging road in the eastern Pennyslvania mountains. Trees passed the door handles in a blur. It seemed a good time to ask, "Muhammad, you afraid of dying?" "You don't ever want to die," he said. I said, "Glad to hear that." Then he went into a wonderful Ali soliloquy: "But the man who built this road is dead now. The man who built that farmhouse over there is dead. There are guys I fought, Sonny Liston, Zora Folley . . . dead . . ."

Good stuff. With video, better. The reporter who avoids today's flip-cam training is a reporter left behind tomorrow. The day Steve Jobs died, a television reporter in Washington, D.C., Neal Augenstein, wrote a tribute of sorts to the Apple genius. He said that since February 2010 he had done all his field production on an iPhone and iPad. No longer did he schlep around a laptop, digital recorders, microphones, cables, video, and still camera.

"No more carrying heavy equipment, waiting for a laptop to boot up or transferring files from a recorder to an editing device," Augenstein wrote. "Now when I leave the relative peace and convenience of the newsroom, my tools to cover news in the nation's capital are an iPhone, iPad and a charger."

The strangest happened, he said.

"Having a tool that facilitates multi-platform reporting." He could shoot video, snap pictures, tweet them immediately, write a story for the station's website. And it "frees a reporter from the challenges of technology to concentrate on storytelling."

As Augenstein has done, every reporter should become his own video editor. Learn web design. Be funny on Twitter, post links to your own stuff, post links to all the good stuff you learned from. Do a blog explaining your processes. Here's what an old sportswriter did as a kid—everything that could be done in a newsroom. Here's what today's young sportswriter must do—everything that can be done on your laptop, your BlackBerry, iPhone, iPad, and, especially, on whatever gizmo they invent tomorrow.

To my question—"Is all this good or bad for reporting?"—Wally Matthews wasn't sure. "Well," he said, "it's certainly thorough."

It's thorough in a way that journalists know is not conducive to their best work. It records everything with little regard to context, perspective, or narrative. It's thorough in the way a thousand-piece jigsaw puzzle is thorough; it's all there, you just have to put the pieces together.

Whatever the negatives, such work will be the beating heart of the new mass media. Warren Buffett, who knows about making money, once said that no one ever built an audience without making money from that audience. So journalists know what they must do. Build the brand. Drive traffic. Draw an audience, all the while hoping that someone figures out how to make the money that makes it possible to do journalism at a pace that allows for the thought essential to storytelling.

 The revolution that has splintered our familiar media universe has created thousands of new outlets in global TV networks and the internet. Those outlets exist because, for all the change, there is a constant: people want to know what's happening. Men scratched pictures on cave walls to tell their buddies about big cats out there with big teeth. People need to know their school board's squabbles, when the city will fix their street's potholes, what their commander-in-chief wants done in Afghanistan. And as much as we need news, we need stories. Hearing the drama of daily life, we learn about our world. Telling the stories of our lives, we teach each other how to get through the day.

How best to tell those stories? I think of William Strunk and Red Smith.

My favorite little textbook on writing is *The Elements of Style*. Strunk, a Cornell University professor, wrote it in 1917. Of his many rules of usage, the most important is rule 17: "Omit needless words." *The New Yorker* essayist E.B. White, a Strunk student who did revisions to the book, wrote that Strunk, in teaching, omitted so many words with such eagerness and such relish that he often found himself with nothing more to say and class time to fill. He wriggled out of the predicament by uttering every sentence three times. "When he delivered his oration on brevity to the class," White wrote, "he leaned forward over his desk, grasped his coat lapels in his hands, and, in a husky, conspiratorial voice, said, 'Rule Seventeen. Omit needless words! Omit needless words! Omit needless words!'"

Smith, the great sports columnist, once said, "I made up my mind that every time I sat down to a typewriter, I would slash my veins and bleed and that I'd try to make each word dance."

Those pieces of advice worked a long time ago.

In today's new mass media world, they still work.

Edited by Katy Feddersen

About Dave Kindred

Dave Kindred has been a sportswriter for 45 years, writing for some of the most prominent newspapers and magazines in the country, such as *The Washington Post*. Publishing nine books, Kindred has had the opportunity to interview some of the most prominent sports figures of our time, including Tiger Woods, Bobby Knight, and Muhammad Ali. His job as a reporter has taken him to seven Olympic Games, 39 Super Bowls, 40 World Series, 43 Kentucky Derbies, and 17 Muhammad Ali championship fights. Kindred is also the 1991 winner of the prestigious sportswriting award, the Red Smith Award for lifetime achievement.

Chapter 5

Crafting Radio News

by

Deb Lesser

News on a radio station is probably something that most of us take for granted; it sort of just happens between the songs. We might hear news in the morning while we're getting ready or perhaps in the afternoon on the way home. We could hear national news or news about our town. News is part of the radio landscape. We just expect it.

As a part of radio programming, news serves as both a fresh source of information and as confirmation of information we may already have. Taken together, radio, television, newspapers, websites, and social media often supply the majority of fresh news that we receive in any given day. Examined critically, we see that many of these news sources are repeating each other. Our 24-hour news cycle is hard to sustain without content repetition.

Radio's strength has always been its ability to be local. It's our local radio station that tells us what is happening in our town, where the traffic jams are, and what that winter storm warning really means. That's when radio news becomes real and important to the listener—when they are directly affected.

Considering the Audience

A good story is always compelling and listeners will follow it both on-air and on the station's website. Good stories have strong **news values**. News values help us to decide what stories are worth our time and attention, both as listeners and as reporters.

Timeliness is a very important news value. The timeliness of a story is determined by how recent the events have occurred. A storm or a car accident or an election are timely stories. Some stories are said to have **legs**, meaning the story will unfold over the course of a few days or weeks. For example, a robbery of a local business is news today. Tomorrow, the manhunt continues. The next day, suspects are apprehended. Next week, suspects are charged.

Other stories have a **long arc**, meaning they will continue to unfold over an extended period of time. The governor being arrested on charges will continue on for many weeks as the charges are documented, a trial is set, and witnesses testify, perhaps uncovering even more information.

Another important news value when considering radio news is **significance**. Significance tells us the impact a story will have. How many people are directly affected by this story? Raising property taxes affects all homeowners. Raising tuition affects all students and their parents. Which is more significant? The answer probably depends on what radio station is delivering the story and the audience that station has.

Stories must be both timely and significant. World War II is very significant story, but not exactly timely. A fender bender in the mall parking lot may be a timely story, but isn't really significant. People listen to radio news because it has the ability to be more timely and significant than print and television news, and the radio news writer should always work to fulfill those listener needs.

Structuring Radio News

Radio news is generally structured in a conversational manner. Stories are often just a few sentences long. Newscasts may only contain three to five stories. A tight time frame of three minutes, including a 30-second commercial and sports and weather makes clear and concise writing essential. The specific times may vary from station to station, but the overarching theme of a strict, quick time frame is used throughout commercial radio.

Radio news writers should always write in short, conversational sentences and use the present tense. The most timely stories should always take precedence over other stories. Also, while writing stories, it's important to put the newest information first in each individual story. For example, if a car accident happened yesterday, a reporter wouldn't begin the story by saying, "Two people were in a car accident yesterday on Main Street." Instead, the reporter should present the newest information first by saying, "Two people are recovering today following a car accident yesterday on Main Street." Notice that presenting the most recent information first also organically shifted our writing from being written in the past tense to the present tense.

Finally, all broadcast news writing should include the title of any given person *before* their name and in as few words as possible. For example, instead of saying, "John McHale, Mayor of Normal," as a newspaper writer might write, the radio news writer would identify the mayor as, "Mayor John McHale." Additionally, attribution should always come first in radio news writing. Instead of, "… said Mayor John McHale," the broadcast writer should use, "Mayor John McHale says …"

Use of Sound

News is much more compelling if it includes a **sound bite** or an **actuality** from an expert or witness. Reporters can use sound bites to add credibility and interest to a story. Sound bites should generally be less than 15 seconds and should provide information that the reporter cannot provide, such as a witness' or an authority's statement. "Fire Chief Reggie Redbird says the origin of the fire is under investigation – (add Fire Chief statement here about suspicious nature of fire). WZND will have more as this story develops." At least one story in every newscast should have sound.

Reporters can gather sound for stories without sound by seeking out local experts. A national story about a killer tornado in Texas gets a local angle when the reporter talks to a local storm chaser, the local TV weather person, or a university professor of meteorology.

Inform, Entertain, Persuade, and Keep Your Job!

Radio stations add news to their programming for a variety of reasons. One reason is because programming local news shows community involvement. News also adds credibility to a station for being an active part of the community, and it keeps a station informed of local happenings.

News also provides sponsorship opportunities for advertisers to sponsor the news, weather, traffic, or sports. General managers are always happy to have sponsors for programming. Fresh news first also keeps listeners tuned to a particular station for information on breaking stories, traffic, and weather. Building listener loyalty translates into higher ratings.

Any station's news mission should be clear; discuss the station's news philosophy with the program director and news director. Consider the demographics of the audience. How much news do they want to hear? What kind of news will they find interesting? Each station will have a particular mix of hard news, sports news, and entertainment news they will find appropriate for their audience and format. If a radio news reporter understands and knows what that mix is it will be easier to find the right stories for each newscast.

Mom Said to Share

Most radio stations share news departments with sister stations. Each of these stations will have a different news philosophy. A country station may be much more interested in the NASCAR standings than the rock station is. The light rock station wants to hear about the city council meeting and the Top 40 station wants to hear the high school sports scores. It is very important that reporters are versatile enough to write stories for all formats. Reporters must also be able to rewrite each story and tell it again every half hour or so during morning and afternoon drive. Listeners would lose interest quickly if they not only heard the same stories repeatedly, but those stories also had the same language.

36

Every good news reporter needs a recorder for sound bites and a camera for pictures. All of this can be accomplished with a great smartphone. After a story has been created for use on-air, always make sure to post it on the stations' websites and social media, again remembering the different station formats.

Listeners Connect

Finally, remember that great local radio news helps build the connection a station has with its listeners, and listeners will often help the station out in return. Most people feel like they could call a radio station and talk to a person if they had a request or some information to share. Encourage listeners to call the news tip hotline and it will feel like the station has an extra staff of reporters.

Edited by Steve Suess

About Deb Lesser

Deb Lesser is the Director of Radio for Illinois State University's School of Communication. In addition to the development, conceptualization, and execution of the radio curriculum, Ms. Lesser is also the Faculty Advisor for WZND, Illinois State University's student radio station. During Ms. Lesser's tenure at Illinois State, both the radio program and WZND have grown exponentially and accumulated numerous national, regional, and local awards.

Ms. Lesser has been selected as an ISU Outstanding University Teacher and has received national recognition as Broadcast Advisor of the Year from College Media Advisors. Deb Lesser received both her B.S. and M.S. from Illinois State University.

Chapter 6

Writing for Television News

by

Laura Trendle-Polus

Writing for Television News

As you begin your career writing for television news, you will find that many things can only be learned by exploring the territory. The industry of television news, like every media, is in a constant state of flux as technology, roles, and practices evolve and adapt to our wants and needs. However, there are several aspects of television that will remain as constants in this evolving field. First, when writing television news, you will always need to consider your audience and tailor your messages accordingly. Additionally, telling a good story is the backbone of all writing, and as a skill, will last far beyond any changes in the industry.

Considering Your Audience

There are several potential audiences that you should keep in mind as a television news writer. Although there are multiple audiences, you will likely only be interested in the main one—known as your *target audience.* This is the audience with whom you want your story to have the most resonance and impact. However, there are other audiences that your message will need to go through before it ever has the opportunity to reach your target audience. In television news this can be the anchor, the producer, the newsroom manager, or a combination of these. Everything you write must pass muster with them first. They are the initial gatekeepers on your message's journey to the target audience.

One of the factors that determine your target audience is what program you're writing for. Take for instance a local morning news show. Those watching likely don't have much time or attention to spend watching the news as they are getting ready, so your emphasis would be on providing them with information in short, easily-digestible bursts. Local nightly news shows, on the other hand, typically include more feature length stories, designed primarily to appeal to an audience of educated, employed adults. Furthermore, a network news magazine show may devote the majority of an hour to tell one story really well. The audience here may be avid news viewers or those drawn by effective promotion during the previous days. Additional factors may be at work too, such as programming to a female audience when a competing station is running a sports event.

To tell your story well you must know your audience. This will come from experience, but you can also get to know your audience by asking some (seemingly) basic questions about them. For instance, does your audience have a history with this story? Would they likely come in with prior knowledge? Does the story resonate with your target audience in a specific way? For example, would placing a story about a cancer survivor in the newscast that follows an Oprah episode on Lance Armstrong be appropriate? Does the story have geographic impact on your target audience? Is it happening close to them? Does the story have other impacts on your target audience? For example, the economic impact of bad news from the largest employer in your area. These are just a few of many questions that you might ask yourself about adapting the message to your target audience. Put yourself in the shoes of target audience members and get to know them and what they want.

Intended Message

The idea you are attempting to share with the audience is your intended message. You will find that this message has a lot of facets as you craft it. The first of these is determining what news function you would like your story to have. Let's begin.

You will want to know your target audience, as discussed. After you know your target audience, the intended function of your story can be chosen. Here we are using a very liberal interpretation of the word "chosen" because typically, if not always, your story exists to *inform* the audience. Persuasion and entertainment are also functions of television news, but with some caveats. Persuasion, or more specifically, deceitful manipulation of your audience, is in fact discouraged. News should be presented objectively, without the presenter taking a side, espousing a specific point of view, or making a call to action. Typically we think of this in terms of not endorsing a candidate, or not speaking out on controversial issues such as abortion or gun control.

However, there are more subtle instances where television newswriters can lapse innocently and inappropriately into persuasive mode. For example, a reporter concludes a live shot at a local jazz festival by urging the audience to come down and enjoy the music. Alternatively, in the tag to a story about a fund-raiser at a local animal shelter, an anchor wishes the group success. Why would an anchor or reporter do this? It is neither the role of the anchor, nor of the reporter, to support such things. Additionally, in teases and promos persuasion is not only acceptable, but it is crucial. Good TV newswriters must understand how to appeal to the audience so that they stay tuned for later stories or parts of a series.

Much like persuasion, entertainment, although not the primary function of news, has increasingly become an integral part of television newswriting. A newscast is like a good meal, with meat and potatoes, vegetables, and a desert. Journalists feel obligated to provide the meat and potatoes (the basics), and the vegetables (the things the audience needs to know for its own good). But the dessert (the funny or touching stories) is what likely keeps the audience coming back for more. So what makes the audience want to consume your message?

The audience will want to watch a television news story based on two general principles: their *need* to know and their *want* to know. Needing to know includes stories that touch on the news values of proximity, prominence, magnitude, timeliness, or usefulness, whereas wanting to know typically includes the news value of novelty. These various news values will determine what stories will make up a newscast. The stories an audience needs to know will come first, followed by increasingly less important, but typically more entertaining, stories. The next time you sit down to watch a newscast analyze the stories and see how closely the station follows this pattern.

News stories, much like newscasts, will lead with the most important information first. You probably know of this as the inverted pyramid style of writing. The first thing must hook the audience so they stick around for the rest of the story.

This device is called a "lead" and is easily one of the most important parts of your story. Audience members are active in their media consumption, so do not expect them to stick around if your story lacks attention-getting words or visuals, or fails to provide them with the information they want. When was the last time you stuck around and watched a news story that was bland or boring from the start?

One last thing about target audiences: they are not random. Typically they are habitual viewers of a certain station, newscast, or program. If you ask most young adults they will tell you the "best" news is on the station their parents or even grandparents always watch, even when the faces change. News stations count on audience members to develop viewing habits based on the programs surrounding the newscast.

Writing Well

One of the overriding characteristics of broadcast writing is that it MUST be clear to the audience viewing or listening. *Clarity* is arguably one of the most important aspects of newswriting. If the message isn't clear, your audience will find one that is and you will lose them. Writing clearly involves combining a direct, conversational style of writing with appropriate and interesting visuals. Additionally, writing in *active voice* is a must. In active voice, your subject acts upon the object. Your sentences must contain a subject, a verb, and an object—preferably in that order. On top of writing clearly and using active voice, there are some stylistic and structural considerations that one needs to keep in mind when writing for television news.

Stylistic conventions may vary slightly so the best way to determine what to use is to simply *ask your boss*. He or she will tell you exactly how things are done at the station you are working at. Typically though, there are some rules-of-thumb that are followed in the industry. First, when it comes to things such as proper names, you will want to use them sparingly. Too many proper names can overload your audience and be confusing—both of which are enemies of clarity. To avoid this, try using relevant descriptors instead—for example saying "A Bloomington mother of two" as opposed to the woman's full name. For names and ages, retain clarity by using "the 37-year-old-woman" as opposed to "the woman, 37." Titles can be crafted much in the same way.

For instance say "ISU President Al Bowman" and not "Al Bowman, President of ISU." This provides clarity to the talent and your audience, and allows you to use four words instead of five—thus saving time. When attributing information remember to use active voice. If the police said that the shooting was accidental, do not say, "the shooting was accidental, say police," instead use, "police say the shooting was accidental."

As mentioned earlier, your target audience is not the only audience that you are writing for. Keep in mind that as a television newswriter you will often be writing copy for someone else to read—typically the anchor or talent. Stylistic conventions are incredibly important in these cases where you will be writing for someone else. Your story must be clear, easy to understand, and also easy to read. If there are misinterpretations between your story and the talent, then you risk losing clarity. Remember, if your story isn't clear, the audience will find one that is. Thus we must follow these stylistic guidelines when writing for news.

To facilitate clarity, we must write things as they are to be said. This means sacrificing space to type out certain words, phrases, or acronyms, so the talent more easily reads them. For example, instead of typing, "23" you would write "twenty-three." Courtesy titles should be spelled out as well (doctor, not Dr.). Any proper names that need pronunciation should be written out phonetically. Symbols such as $ and % should be avoided and written out instead. Abbreviations such as "lbs" should be written out as well ("pounds"). Additionally, acronyms such as "ISU" or "NAACP" should be written as they are said ("I-S-U" and "N-double-A-C-P").

Another one of these stylistic conventions is that news is written in a split page format. Technical directions for the director and crew appear on the left side, whereas the right side will contain all of the text to be read by the anchor, or talent. Luckily, newsroom software will usually format this way for you. There are five basic forms that news will follow, each with its own conventions and formats. These are Readers (RDR), Voiceover (VO), Voiceover/Sound on Tape (VO/SOT), Package (PKG), and Live Shot (LIVE). There will be slight variations in each of these depending on the station you work for, so again, remember to ask your boss regarding exact stylistic details.

Strong, effective television news stories must be concise, correct, and complete. A typical local "newshole" is 10 to 12 minutes. Thus broadcasters try and fit as many stories in to that time frame as possible. High story counts are desirable. Stories must be concise to fit in. Additionally, audiences are considered to have short attention spans, so each aspect of the newscast (stories, sound bites, reporter tracks, and so forth) is as short as possible. Television newswriters will do many things to be concise. Putting the most important information first, such as leading with the result of the news event, is one way of doing this. We have discussed active voice already, and this tool helps cut out unnecessary words and saving time. To be even more concise, consider eliminating wordy transitions or introductory clauses. Actively trying to be concise will train you to choose facts carefully, by removing all of the nonessential information. However, this must be done without sacrificing correctness.

In addition to being concise, television news reports must be correct. Imagine the consequences involved if newscasters made erroneous reports. Wrong information may cause the audience to react in inappropriate or potentially dangerous ways. Wrong information also has the potential to damage the story subject's reputation, may open the station to legal action, and can damage the reporter's, anchor's, station's, and industry's reputation and credibility. Reporting on important stories requires hard work. Phone calls, double-checking facts and sources, and tracking down additional viewpoints are all things that can assist in crafting a correct story. When writing it, make sure you are reading it aloud so you have a chance to hear how it will sound when broadcasted. Then revise it. Read aloud again, and have others read your copy. Then revise it again.

Writing Good Stories Well

We must keep a lot of things in mind when writing. Your audience, message intent, clarity, and stylistic conventions are just a few of the many things that must be considered when writing a television news story. Another element of good stories is drama. While one might argue that television news is not a typical story, you simply need to take a look at any newscast to see that any good story within it will typically include dramatic elements. Protagonists, a will or a want, a realization, complications, a climax, and resolutions are easily identified in most good news stories. Check out nearly every political story, disaster report, or sports story for examples of this. While dramatic structure will not inherently make a story good, they should be kept in mind as well.

Writing television news well is not something we just do—it is a process—and it is one that takes time, dedication, skill, and passion.

Edited by Adam Rahn

About Laura Trendle-Polus

Laura Trendle-Polus currently teaches broadcast reporting and media writing courses at Illinois State University. In addition, she is the News Director for the award-winning TV-10 News program at Illinois State University. Laura earned both her B.S. and M.S. from Illinois State University. Prior to teaching, she won several awards for her breaking coverage of the Jeffrey Dahmer serial killings in the early 1990s.

Chapter 7
Copywriting for Television
by
Dr. Brent K. Simonds

Writing Careers

Creating local television advertising is often where many aspiring writers begin their careers. Employment opportunities include advertising agencies, video production companies, and television stations. Depending on the size of your broadcast market, you may find yourself in professional roles beyond writing such as shooting, editing, and graphics/animation creation. Typically, as you move up the career ladder or into larger markets, you will find that a higher degree of specialization is expected. However, the focus of this essay is on writing and to create value for clients by creating strategic and creative media messages. Furthermore, your job expectations will be shaped by the type of organization for which you work (e.g., agency vs. station).

For example, television stations air three different types of non-program material: commercials (spots), promotions (promos), and public service announcements (PSAs). Commercials are paid placements that advertise goods and services for a profit-driven business. Promos are promotional placements that stations produce and air to "sell" their own product. For example, a promo might highlight what is coming up on the local news, or may tout how the station scooped its competitors on a recent story (called proof of performance, or POP). Finally, a public service announcement may "advertise" the goods and services of a non-profit agency or other charity. The PSA is given free air time by the station, though it is **not** typically during high ratings programming such as primetime.

If you work for an advertising agency you will, of course, write lots of television commercials and some PSAs (if your agency does pro bono work), but probably will never create promos for local stations. The same goes for a copywriter at a video production company, though it might be possible to work on large promotional efforts for a local station, especially if your company has high end or niche skills that may be lacking at local stations. A writer at a television station may be engaged in all three forms, with promos constituting much of the work.

Advertising Agencies

Advertising agencies work with their clients to create strategies for promoting their businesses and helping them sell goods and services. This includes creating ads as well as buying and placing those ads in a variety of media. Therefore, full-service ad agencies deal with areas outside of television such as radio, newspapers, magazines, billboards, and websites (unless the agency has a niche specialty). Therefore, a copywriter at an agency may be called upon to write copy for several media. Furthermore, clients who use ad agencies typically spend a lot of money on advertising and they may be a little more sophisticated with what they require. For example, they may have different spots that air in different day parts using different strategies to target the particular audience that is watching that programming.

Thus, agency copywriters will need to work closely with creative directors and account executives so that the message they write hews closely with the overall strategy the agency and the client is pursuing. This means that the ad copy needs to work in each medium it is intended for and compliments the other efforts. It is common for a radio or television commercial to mention print ads or websites. For maximum impact, all of these messages should be integrated gracefully.

Depending on the agency, actual production of the spot may be handled by someone else, such as freelancers, production companies, or TV stations. However, since the agency is carefully managing the message they will maintain creative control of the production.

Of course, copywriters are always constrained by budget. It makes no sense to dream up a commercial worthy of the Super Bowl when the client is not willing or is unable to spend the money necessary to realize your creative vision. Remember that there are two main things that businesses are paying agencies for: creative services and strategic placement. That is, they have to pay to produce the commercial and then to air the commercial. Airtime is by far where most of the budget goes on a local spot. It does not make much sense to spend most of your budget on creative production and then not have enough money left over to buy enough airtime to be effective.

Also, it is important to understand how agencies make money. A large part of the money made by agencies is through what is called the "agency discount." What this means is that a broadcast station will automatically discount the price of the air buy (typically 15%) when it is placed by an agency rather than directly by the business. For example, let's say a local mom and pop shop have $10,000 to buy airtime on their local network affiliate. If the business places the air buy directly with the station it will cost them $10,000. If they hire an agency, it still costs the shop $10,000 but it only costs the agency $8,500. The agency pockets $1,500 and everyone is happy because Mom and Pop get professional guidance for "free." Right?

Well, this is where writing and production of the commercial comes in. How much will it cost to produce the spot? Is the agency willing to do the creative for "free" or will they do it for "cost" or will they go all out and "mark up" the production in order to create another revenue stream? While it may sound like the mom and pop shop cannot go wrong with an agency, it may not be the direction they should take. For one thing, unless the shop is planning on spending lots of money on advertising for an extended period, agencies might not want to take them as a client. That is, small budgets over a short period of time might not make it worthwhile for the agency. Furthermore, if the mom and pop shop are only interested in television advertising and not radio, newspaper, magazine, billboards, and web; it might make better sense to deal directly with the television station and their account executives, writers, and production staff.

Because of the agency discount, some businesses that have large local advertising budgets (e.g., car dealerships) may create in-house agencies. This agency is set up as separate business from the main business, but it only has one client. The business then may only need one or two people to handle the creative and make the air buys and then pocket the savings from the discount. Again, this only makes sense for a company that consistently spends lots of money on local advertising (enough to support the agency employees and overhead, while still saving enough money to justify having the in-house operation).

Production Companies

Production companies differ from ad agencies in that they typically are not involved in buying airtime or placing ads. They are hired for their creative expertise with producing quality audio and video messages. Consequently, production companies may be involved with many projects beyond producing 30-second commercials. A production company could be hired to write, shoot, and edit several videos for a company to serve diverse purposes. For example, the production company could produce a series of 30-second spots to air locally, a five-minute "history" of its client's business for its website, and a DVD with product demonstrations that its client might use in a trade show booth. So, unlike the writer at the ad agency who might write copy for TV, radio, newspaper, or magazine ads, the writer at a video production company may be writing only for video albeit for different lengths and purposes. Since there is no revenue stream from placing ads, production companies must rely on clients paying for creative production services. For this reason, production companies are typically involved with clients who are willing to pay for higher production values. However, budgets still matter so writers must create ideas that can be realized with the money available.

Production companies are sometimes contracted by ad agencies to produce the spots the agency writer has created. In this case, creative control is generally with the agency, though a good production company will add value to the spot with its particular expertise.

Some production companies may also work on PSAs pro bono. In fact, many ad agencies and production companies may produce work each year for local non-profits as a way of being good community citizens.

Television Stations

Writers at local television stations who are not involved in news operations work in departments known variously as creative services, promotions, or marketing. Stations in smaller markets may create commercials for their clients who buy airtime, but in larger markets this is usually not the case. Larger television markets have a greater number of ad agencies and production companies available that handle these roles than do smaller markets. However, promotions writers/producers at television stations can be found in every market since agencies and production companies do not typically handle station promos.

At a local station that provides creative services for commercial production, clients may be referred to as either "agency" or "direct." The station may produce a commercial written by the agency or merely air a commercial provided to them by an agency. A direct client means that the business is relying on the station to provide an on-air strategy plus creative services.

More often than not, if you work at a station in a creative services department, the clients you encounter typically do not have large advertising budgets. Otherwise, they would use an ad agency or perhaps have an in-house agency. It really depends on the market you find yourself in. Consequently, you may be dealing with new businesses or businesses that have not bought television advertising before. Also, because the main service the station is providing the client is airtime, not as much money may be set aside in the budget for creative services as there would be at a production company. So, a writer in creative services for a local station has to find a way to create a message effectively and inexpensively.

If writers are involved with station promotions they may find themselves—like their ad agency counterparts—writing for radio, newspaper, and the web because many television stations promote their on-air product in those media.

Strategies

The goal for any business that purchases commercial airtime on a local station is to increase sales of goods and services. However, this may be accomplished directly or indirectly. And, even though the main goal is to increase revenue, clients may have other motivations as well. If you want to successfully create messages for your clients, you will want to explore their motivations.

If you are dealing with clients that have a long history of advertising in the area, you will want to pay close attention to what they have created in the past. For example, many family-owned businesses may go back several generations (even past the beginning of television in the late 1940s/early 1950s). Businesses such as these have strong name recognition and probably have a slogan that local residents know by heart. They have a strong sense of identity in the community that has been honed through decades of advertising. Do not mess with success. Often these business owners appear in their own commercials and have become—through years of exposure

—"celebrities." Do not let this motivation escape you. They probably enjoy their celebrity and if you get to write copy for them, keep this in mind. This might be something you should try pitching to new clients, too. If the business owner is recognized in public, it might be a strong motivator to purchase more airtime.

If you are writing for new advertisers you do not have an historical precedent to know how they want to represent themselves to the public. This is why you need to spend time with the client and ask lots of questions. Who are their customers or who do they want them to be? Is the business appealing to all ages or to a targeted demographic? Do they want to be perceived as hip and cutting edge or would they prefer to appear authoritative and trustworthy. In other words, are they selling skateboards or insurance?

Since, at the end of the day, a commercial is striving to be persuasive, what action are you trying to motivate? Sometimes it may be very direct such as a commercial that depicts a series of prices/items that are on sale through Friday at a local hardware store. The motivation for the consumer is that it is a good deal and that it is not always going to be that price. This is called a scarcity appeal. Obviously, you need shots of the products and graphics with prices plus business name, logo, and location. This is very cut and dried, but it works and is easy to write and produce.

This might be a great strategy for a store that sells goods, but it would not be appropriate for a service-oriented business. For example, how about a local attorney who specializes in personal injury claims? You are not trying to motivate someone to come buy the service and visit the law office before Friday. Rather you are trying to motivate the person to call the law office if injured on the job. Obviously, you are qualifying the prospective client—"if you have been injured you may not be getting everything coming to you." Then, motivating the person to call means that the phone number needs to be repeated both aurally and visually several times. This is a good time to mention, too, how important the placement is for particular messages. It makes much more sense to air this spot during the day rather than primetime since the air rates would be so much cheaper, plus your intended audience (the injured) is sitting at home watching television, the law office is open, and someone is there to take the call.

So, armed with the necessary copy points and the business name/logo/slogan/jingle these types of spots are formulaic and easy to write—but they work. Just be sure that you have identified which action you are trying to motivate. It could be a store visit, phone call, or a website visit. Your job is to equip the audience to take the desired action.

A price/item spot with sale dates and the hardware store's location may appeal to the bargain seeker, but what if you are trying to sell a top-of-the-line lawn mower that is never on sale? How do you motivate the consumer of high-end products? This is when images can speak much louder than words.

As a writer in a visual medium you are also specifying what people see, not just the words they hear. If fact, several successful commercials have very little spoken words at all. In this case, instead of a shot of a lawnmower in the foreground with a graphic of the price, how about slow motion footage of a toddler and puppies on a perfectly manicured lawn with a beautiful sunset? Dad is setting in the shade while mom brings him lemonade. Warm, nostalgic music plays. End with a shot of a gleaming, overpriced riding mower with the store logo superimposed. Fade to black.

This is referred to as "presentational" rather than "propositional." Propositional statements are either true or false (e.g., "This is the price until Friday"). Whereas, the image of the toddler and puppies on the beautiful lawn is presentational—it just is. No overt "truth claim" is made and thus the image cannot be judged as true or false. You are not appealing to the audience's intellect; you are trying to trigger their emotions. Do not underestimate the ability of the audience's emotions to motivate action.

Writing successful copy for television is predicated on writers understanding their clients, their audiences, and their medium. There should be a clearly identified strategy that the message you craft is poised to fulfill. Remember, it is a business first, and a creative outlet second.

So, if you find yourself in a beginning copywriter position it will probably be at an ad agency, production company, or television station. Though the type and scope of the work may differ depending on where you are employed, the goals will always be the same: to create value for businesses by being creative.

Edited by Richard Green

About Brent K. Simonds

Dr. Brent K. Simonds is an Associate Professor of Communication at Illinois State University. Before becoming a professor he spent 14 years as a director and producer of various broadcast programs, as well as educational and instructional films. Simonds has won various national awards for his work including the Telly Award for the instructional video *Leading Instructional Discussions*.

Chapter 8

Mass Media Writing and the Public Relations Major

by

Peter M. Smudde, Ph.D., APR

and

Jeffrey L. Courtright, Ph.D.

The U.S. Department of Labor's Bureau of Labor Statistics' *Occupational Outlook Handbook 2010-2011* says, "Employment of public relations specialists is expected to grow 24 percent from 2008 to 2018, much faster than the average for all occupations." This kind of growth has characterized the field for years because the need for highly competent professional communicators is ever present, especially with the increasing competition in every industry and the global business environment.

Special attention within the public relations field is on professionals who possess knowledge of other languages and cultures. But most important for students enrolled in COM 161 is the great need for additional expertise in the prudent and effective use of communication technology, including social media, which can carry messages that inspire cooperation between organizations and their publics.

Our students graduate from ISU's public relations program very well prepared for their careers as knowledgeable, competent, prudent, and active professionals who add value to the organizations for which they work. Our students' academic, research, and service experiences continue to enrich their lives and those of the ISU community. In COM 161, your study of and practice with electronic and social media shall especially fit the matters of enacting public relations strategies, handling the writing process, designing appropriate and effective messages, and choosing to use the best media for public relations purposes and audiences.

Strategic Planning Defines the Big Picture

In business and, indeed, public relations, strategy is key, and the word "strategy" is often paired with "planning." The true art of developing relations with publics is when organizations' and their publics' interests and needs truly mesh for mutual benefits. That meshing of organizational and audience needs and interests must be understood well before any PR text can be written.

The outputs of public relations must have a larger yield than the gratification gained immediately upon their release. PR outputs are "tactics"—the final products—of a thorough strategic plan for what an organization wants to accomplish through its communication. As the "father" of public relations, Edward L. Bernays, wrote in his book, *Public Relations* (1958), "Do not think of tactics in terms of segmental approaches. The problem is not to get articles into a newspaper or obtain radio time or arrange for a motion-picture newsreel; it is, rather, to set in motion a broad activity, the success of which depends on interlocking all phases and elements of the proposed strategy, implemented by tactics that are timed to the moment of maximum effectiveness" (p. 167).

Effective public relations—the measured and ethical use of language and symbols to inspire cooperation between an organization and its publics—comes through an astute combination of strategic thinking and skillful communication in any medium. This combination is essential among the best practitioners. But public relations professionals (students also) too often jump to tactics: what was used in the past worked well or is the hot, new trend, so it must be the right thing to do in the present. (All the hype around the use of social media in public relations is a good example.) More important on this point is this: Public relations professionals who jump to tactics probably only understand discourse conventions (i.e., the rules for writing and designing texts) at a surface level, and deeper understanding of discourse conventions within the context of the "big picture" would better inform their thinking to be more strategic and, presumably, more successful. Form must follow function. Alternatively, tactics must follow from a sound strategy.

Writing Process Demands

Public relations is a very writing-intensive field. Everyone who works in it is expected to be an exemplary communicator in all forms—written, spoken, and mediated. Because you would be paid to be the best communicator in an organization, you must produce high-quality work well within tight deadlines. *This expectation also includes adherence to the rules of proper English grammar and mechanics, Associated Press (AP) style, and document design.* Therefore, you must learn those rules thoroughly and apply them accurately, because your livelihood and professional reputation depends greatly on your skillfulness as a writer, speaker, and overall communicator. You must be good at it all the time in every way.

So much more is demanded of effective public relations than the mere final product of one's or a group's work to bring a text into being for specific audiences and particular purposes. Effective public relations requires sound process *and* product, the latter being the result of the former. At the same time, though, the type of public relations discourse that is the focus of the process of bringing it into being plays a role in its creation. The process of creating any public relations discourse is governed by a combination of personal and organizational procedures. That writing process, too, must be in tune with a sound strategy to inspire cooperation between an organization and its publics.

Your work in COM 161 is a major step in building your skillfulness in the various kinds of public relations discourse that is the real driving force in the process of planning, developing, producing, and evaluating effective communication between an organization and its publics. This idea means basically that skillfulness (also called "discourse competence") is the reason that public relations professionals and students can strategize about and accomplish what they must to be successful at their work for both their organizations and their publics.

Message Design

To students taking COM 161, a poorly written press release should be obvious. Hallmarks are bad grammar and spelling, poor or no application of AP style, inaccurate statements of facts, use of hyperbole ("hype") to sell rather than inform, broken discourse conventions for no apparent reason, and so on.

Well-written news stories are a cohesive statement of the organization's perspective on a situation, thus preserving in print, audio, or visual form that particular perspective (i.e., it becomes part of the historical record). News stories in any form offer unique opportunities that their framing and organizational patterns provide.

In contrast to their journalistic roots, PR texts invite strategic opportunities for identity management. PR news texts, by defining the organization and, at least implicitly, the audience through discourse, allows organizations to articulate relationships between themselves and their publics in the sense that the persona and values it presents invites publics to identify with the organization and those values.

Media Selection and Measurement

Contrary to what many people believe, the medium is *not* the message—medium *and* message work together in ways that organizations use to inspire cooperation with their audiences while also inviting them to celebrate their common ground. As Marshall McLuhan (1964) argues, "the message of any medium or technology [itself] is the change of scale or pace or pattern that it introduces into human affairs" (p. 24). The medium and message are necessarily bound together, as the medium/form of communication follows from the reason/function for what is said. Messages and their purposes affect media choices, and media literally shape the messages in space and time.

The strategic use of public relations text types (also called "discourse genres") takes place within the context of communication campaigns. As we argue in our book, any of the many types of PR discourse may be used to increase awareness, change attitudes, and/or obtain certain behaviors. Any PR discourse genre also may be used in combination, for example, in crisis communication (Smudde & Courtright, 2012). Product introduction campaigns, for example, may utilize many different kinds of PR discourse, but together enact the characteristics and functions of campaign rhetoric to heighten awareness about a product, inspire favorable opinions about it and the organization that made it, and inspire people to buy it.

Conclusion

Your study of journalistic, public relations, and social media writing is a vital starting point in developing your skillfulness in today's and, especially, tomorrow's communication environment. A strong theoretical and the practical background in professional communication is essential for you to be successful in your career. The intersection of your study in COM 161 with public relations' strategy, writing process, message design, and media selection should pay off in the short term as you continue your studies and in the long term as you embark on a career in public relations.

Edited by Sarah Haynes

About Pete Smudde

Pete Smudde is an Associate Professor and the PR Program Coordinator at Illinois State University's School of Communication. He has 25 years of experience (16 of them in the industry), a master's degree from Illinois State University, a doctoral degree from Wayne State University, as well as accreditation in public relations through PRSA. Dr. Smudde's research interests include public relations' role in and contributions to corporate strategy, analytical approaches to public relations and organizational communication, leadership and management matters for organizations, the connections between network science and word-of-mouth promotion, and pedagogical approaches to public relations that meet academic and industry demands.

About Jeffrey Courtright

Jeffrey Courtright is an Assistant Professor at Illinois State University's School of Communication. Dr. Courtright obtained a master's degree from the University of Louisiana at Lafayette and a doctoral degree from Purdue University. His research interests center on the relationship between public relations message design and organizational reputation.

References

Bernays, E. L. (1952). *Public relations*. Norman, OK: University of Oklahoma Press.

McLuhan, M. (1964). *Understanding media: The extensions of man* (2nd ed). New York: Mentor/Penguin.

Smudde, P. M., & Courtright, J. L. (2012). *Inspiring cooperation & celebrating organizations: Genres, message design & strategies in public relations*. New York: Hampton Press.

U.S. Department of Labor, Bureau of Labor Statistics. (2011). *Occupational outlook handbook, 2010-11 edition*. Retrieved from http://www.bls.gov/oco/

Chapter 9: The Recursive Documentary Writing Process

The Case of *Pontiac's Rebellion*

by

John P. McHale, Ph.D. and Brian Seay

Del Griffith, *Planes, Trains, and Automobiles:* "You just go with the flow. Like a twig on the shoulders of a mighty stream."

—*Planes, Trains, and Automobiles* (1987)

The documentary writer, like Del Griffith, the shower curtain ring guy in John Hughes's film *Planes, Trains, and Automobiles* (1987) played by John Candy, must roll with the flow of what footage can be shot and the evolution of a story.

Nonfiction film composition is a constantly changing process. It involves writing, and rewriting countless drafts and generating dozens of ideas. And a lot of times you have to scrap a lot of those ideas. But sometimes, the subject matter you've chosen can bring you magic. Regardless, it's imperative that one goes with the flow when writing documentary films. "Like a twig on the shoulders of a mighty stream."

In this chapter, we identify the story that evolved during the production of Brian Seay's *Pontiac's Rebellion*. Seay wrote, directed, produced, and coedited *Pontiac's Rebellion* (2009) and McHale served as the executive producer on this documentary film project.

In this chapter, we review relevant literature, establish a method which we use as an analytical lens through which we study this case, describe our findings, and conclude with a summary of the most relevant findings. This case study provides an indicative example of how writing and producing a documentary on a local political issue is a cyclical process.

Documentary writers can and should develop an initial plan, but they must always be cognizant of the changing nature of the story—which is based on real life events. We will focus on that evolution through initial concept formulation, writing the treatment, constructing a shot wish list, amending the plan while shooting, and revising the story in editing.

Documentaries on Political Activism

Although little research has been afforded the production of documentaries on political issue campaign activity, much work has been done on the effects of the media in general. The concern that media, such as film, could have strong effects on people began with the philosophical and sociological consideration of the unique characteristics of industrialized mass society (Durkheim, 1933; Tönnies, 1940) and continued through the study of the media's use of propaganda (Hovland, Janis, & Kelly, 1953; Lasswell, 1935; Lippmann, 1922). Research on the impact of the media subsequently moved toward an assumption of limited effects (Janis et al., 1959; Katz & Lazarsfeld, 1955; Klapper, 1960; Lazarsfeld & Merton, 1948; Schramm, 1954; Schramm, Lyle, & Parker, 1961), with scholars generally concluding that the media could have some effect when their messages were consistent with those from other socializing groups (e.g., family and peers) and institutions (e.g., education and religion).

This type of media effects research, conducted in a mainstream, social-scientific tradition in the United States (e.g., the early work of Lazarsfeld and others), stood in sharp contrast to an alternate approach, largely European in origin, that started with the early work of the Frankfurt School, followed by later research linked to the British cultural studies tradition (e.g., Adorno, 1991; Fiske & Hartley, 1978; Fromm, 1976; Hall, 1982; Marcuse, 1964), which focused on the ideological role of the media. These explorations of media ideology assume people experience prolonged media exposure to ideological positions that are consistent with other cultural influences. Perhaps because of this influence, a move towards viewing the media as having moderate effects (more impact than assumed under a limited effects perspective but less than originally assumed by the strong effects perspective) arose in the United States after the 1960s in theoretical perspectives such as social learning theory (Bandura, 1971), agenda setting (McCombs & Shaw, 1972), spiral of silence (Noelle-Neumann, 1984), and cultivation analysis (Gerbner, 1999). Accompanying research demonstrated that long-term exposure to ubiquitous media frequently produced significant influences on individuals. Little of this research, however, focused on the production process of activist activity on a local political issue.

Some work has been done on the impact of political film. Feldman and Sigelman (1985), for instance, studied the effects of the television film *The Day After*, about midwestern U.S. survivors of a hypothetical nuclear war between the United States and the Soviet Union, finding that viewers reported learning more about the possible implications of nuclear war but did not change their opinions about what policies would best avoid such a conflict. Lenart and McGraw (1989), however, did find that U.S. citizens who viewed *Amerika*, a made-for-television film about a fictional invasion of the United States by Soviet military forces and their Central American allies, demonstrated an increase in conservative views about relations between the United States and the Soviet Union. These two studies were sensitive to the context in which viewers saw these films (such as if they watched them with other people or the location where they watched them), but they did not focus on the writing and production of video/film documentary about activists.

There also is a rich tradition of scholarship on the use of media by activists (e.g., Goodman, 2003; Nichols, 1981, 1991, 1994; Ryan, 1991; Ryan, Carragee, & Schwerner, 1998), although little exists on the use of documentary video/film for that purpose. The lack of such research is unfortunate, for there is a history of using video/film documentary as a vehicle for social protest and reform. For instance, John Grierson used film documentary in Britain in the 1920s and 1930s to raise public consciousness about social problems, and his work was influential in the creation of a number of subsequent documentaries on social conditions in Great Britain and the impact of imperialism abroad (Barnouw, 1993). The documentary film work of Pare Lorentz in the United States during the 1930s, including *The Plow that Broke the Plains* (1936) and *The River* (1937), promoted social change by highlighting problems of rural poverty. On the other side of the political spectrum, the Nazis used documentary film, most notably the work of Leni Riefenstahl (e.g., *Triumph of the Will*), to promote their agenda in Europe. In more recent years, filmmakers such as Errol Morris (*Thin Blue Line* and *Fog of War*) and Michael Moore (*Roger and Me, Bowling for*

Columbine, and *Fahrenheit 9/11*) have promoted progressive agendas through their films.

Although there has been little study of the political or social impact of video/film documentaries, there have been considerable critical analyses of such work, such as Bohn's (1977) study of the films from the U.S. World War II documentary series *Why We Fight*. Much of this work has been text-based, engaging in close readings/analyses of the content and form of specific documentaries, but frequently not examining issues related to the influence of these documentaries. One exception is Reeves (1999), who found that propaganda films that were consistent with previously held views had more impact on viewers than propaganda films that were inconsistent with audience members' preconceptions.

Little work has been done, however, on the writing and production of documentary video/film by activists engaged in political campaign, like that in the case of the prison in Pontiac, Illinois. A notable exception is Whiteman (2004), who studied the relationship between documentary films and several social movements seeking reform, including a documentary that pushed for better public housing in North Carolina, one that exposed social and environmental hazards linked to mining in Wisconsin and how that documentary was used by environmental groups, and how labor activists used a documentary on textile production in the southeastern United States that examined a bitter and violent strike in the 1930s that had long been neglected as a political resource. From this analysis, Whiteman developed a coalition model of political impact to better understand the role of documentary film designed to promote social justice issues. According to this model, the impact of an activist documentary is best studied by examining its development, production, and distribution stages, something that past research had neglected. Whiteman also contended that past research employed an "individualistic model" that focused on the influence of film documentaries on individuals' attitudes and behaviors, and he argued for the need to study the broader influence of documentaries on reforms and policies being sought by social movements.

McHale (2006) examined the development, production, and distribution stages of the video documentary about Joe Amrine, a man who was on Missouri death row despite no evidence or witnesses against him and the use of the video to help stop the use of the death penalty in the United States. This video documentary was guided by an emergent grounded theory derived from the use of a constant comparison process to analyze ethnographically gathered data (interviews with individuals and focus groups conducted with over 40 activists, field notes from participant observation, and printed materials from activist organizations) about advocacy communication (McHale, 2004). This practical, middle-range perspective identified communication forms used by activists, the intended audiences for this communication, the perceived functions of this communication, and the factors that influence such communication. In particular, the perspective identified video as an especially effective tool of social action for reaching the general public, other activists, politicians, and the media. The theory also revealed that video potentially can achieve a variety of functions, including educating people, mobilizing advocates, aiding lobbying efforts, and facilitating media coverage. This theory also revealed that video/film has particular characteristics—such as multiple cues, language variety (e.g., formal versus casual or the source characteristics of interviewees versus a narrator), and a personal character (e.g., humanizing the topic by showing the individual human beings involved)—that contribute to its effectiveness in reaching and motivating these audiences. This research will inform our study of the writing and production of *Pontiac's Rebellion.*

Method

We explicate the writing and production process of a documentary on a grassroots political campaign in a small town. The purpose of this inquiry is to formulate theory concerning the production of documentary on political advocate activity through qualitative inquiry methods. The practices that are relevant to this study revolve around the effort to keep Pontiac Correctional Center open in Pontiac, Illinois. Communication is a prevalent activity of these advocates. The goal of qualitative study should be the discovery of meaning to those who share a particular situatedness or worldview. In this case, these are the documentarians who sought to gather video and write and produce a documentary on local political efforts. In an effort to ascertain the emic knowledge shared by those who also share a similar life-world, our overarching research question is: How is the process of writing and producing a documentary on a local, grassroots political campaign unique?

We are interested in the pragmatic considerations of writing and producing documentaries on political issue campaigns. The focus of our inquiry is to identify and evaluate the writing and production process. Through a constant comparative method we identify categories of media available to advocates, and I develop theoretical postulates as a result of recursive consideration of composition of categories and the relationships between those categories. We developed theoretical propositions as a result of my effort to develop grounded theory (Glaser & Strauss, 1967; Strauss & Corbin, 1998). Several areas of communication have previously been studied utilizing this method (Benoit, 1997; Fairhurst, 1993; Hart & Williams, 1995; Lange, 1993; Neuliep, 1991; Peterson et al., 1994; Sabourin & Stamp, 1995; Stamp, 1994; Tracy & Baratz, 1993). The rationale for using the Glaser and Strauss method of theory generation is that it allows for the inductive generation of theory. Theory arises from the analysis of data, particularly through the use of the constant comparative method. Data analysis was guided by the philosophical assumptions and practical considerations offered by grounded theory (Glaser & Strauss, 1967; Glaser, 1978; Strauss & Corbin, 1998). Rather than analyze data through existing theory, we aspired to develop theory on documentary production on local political issue activism that is grounded in our data and developed through constant comparative analysis of that data. Thus, constant comparative analysis (Glaser & Strauss, 1967; Strauss & Corbin, 1998) was used to develop a categorical framework of communication of local advocacy activists. My ultimate aim has been to develop theory grounded in analysis of qualitative data generated from ethnographic investigation of social advocates.

The meanings attributed to communication media by documentary writers and producers are the most important data of this study. We focused on documentarians' advocates' perceptions about how a documentary on a local grassroots advocacy campaign is constructed. Perceptions of writing and production effectiveness will be considered in the study. Thus, ethnographic methods of data collection are most appropriate. We worked with local advocates involved in efforts in the issue area; and analyzed data gathered in field notes from over a year of participant observation and recollections of the primary documentary writer and producer. The triangulation of data gathering methods has provided a check against the weaknesses of specific approaches and provided for comparison between data types. This study reveals how documentaries can be constructed on social and political advocate activities.

Findings

The video project first involved researching and crafting the cinematic approach in the pre-production and production stages. The effort then entailed post-production and editing, followed by exhibition showings of the video and other promotional activities.

Concept Formulation

Brian Seay was a student in Communication 351: Long-Form Mass Media Writing, taught by Dr. John P. McHale when he began to write *Pontiac's Rebellion*. Seay first heard of the story while working as a photojournalist at a central Illinois TV station. Rod Blagojevich, governor of Illinois at the time, was planning to close down a state prison in Pontiac, Illinois. Residents of Pontiac were not pleased. The prison was a vital source of jobs and income for the small town. Naturally, the people of Pontiac wanted to keep it open. They held rallies and press events for months to try to combat a December 31, 2008, closure enacted by the governor. Seay began shooting and following key players in the Pontiac community in October, unsure of whether the prison would shutter on the December 31 deadline.

Writing the Treatment

After considering the idea for several weeks, Seay began constructing a treatment. The treatment was a barebones explanation of the story. But the end was uncertain.

The treatment included a title, a synopsis (approximately 50 words), and a four-page narrative of the story Seay hoped to tell in the documentary, assuming he got the required footage. The narrative incorporated footage Seay had already gathered and logged. Logging footage is the process of writing down the location of usable pieces of footage already gathered, generally noting elements every 30 seconds or at points of transition. During the logging process, Seay would note the time code of each element and begin to select shots that would be useful in the finished documentary.

Constructing a Wish List

By the time Seay started diving into the writing of the documentary, he had already started shooting a good amount of video and following around a couple of subjects. But once he started writing, he planned as much as he could. Seay constructed a tentative script incorporating footage he already had and a *wish list* of footage he hoped to obtain. As Seay continued to gather footage, he logged it, then incorporated the usable shots into the script. This is an indicative example of how writing a documentary is a recursive process, as opposed to writing other preplanned, long-form videos or films.

During a discussion session in McHale's Long-Form Mass Media Writing course, Seay outlined the story arc of his documentary on the whiteboard. As part of the development of a full-length screenplay in that course, McHale has each student share the dramatic structure of the evolving script. Obviously, since Seay's long-form program was a documentary rather than a fictional full-length film, it was a unique experience for those in the class. Seay outlined for the group the main protagonists, their will and want, the resulting major dramatic question, the complications faced by the protagonists, and the structure of the three acts. But the third act was completely blank. Unfortunately, at the time of the class discussion, there was no apparent plot point at the end of the second act from which a third act could be constructed. McHale suggested that Seay might have to manipulate the footage and the unfolding plan to find some sort of third act climax for the documentary. Seay faced a challenge.

Amending the Plan During Production

The difference between pre-production and production is less distinct in video/film documentary than with other types of media programming because of the dependence in documentaries on occurrences that are videotaped or filmed as they happen.

Once Seay structured a tentative shooting schedule, he confirmed taping plans with the principals involved and made arrangements for locations. Even the construction of the shooting schedule was flexible, with plans amended to accommodate participants and locations.

Initially, in the production stage, a number of interviews had to be conducted. Interviews with the mayor of Pontiac were critical to the project. Seay set up shooting dates and interviewed him several times. The footage from that interview was compelling and became an important part of our final product.

Seay also wanted to give those on the other side an opportunity to share counterfactuals of which we were not aware. This decision was linked to his commitment to provide balance in the video documentary rather than a desire to include conflict in the documentary narrative. Research also suggests that audiences may be more receptive to a presentation that offers arguments from both sides of an issue (see, e.g., Allen, 1998).

Illinois State University School of Communication was a supportive environment for the production, dissemination, and promotion of the video documentary. The university and its School of Communication offered logistical support for the project; in particular, equipment and technical knowledge provided by School of Communication faculty and staff provided support for production of Seay's documentary. Seay had access to the necessary equipment and personnel with specialized computer skills and other requisite knowledge, and the opportunity to work with other students also was helpful. Seay's professor, McHale, even cosigned on a bank loan so Seay could buy a top-quality camera for the project.

The production of the video documentary added energy to activists fighting to save the prison and increased their morale, as was the case to a more limited extent during pre-production, which is consistent with Whiteman's (2004) findings. The few activists who had been working on the case felt validated by the existence of the documentary.

On December 9, 2008, executive producer McHale was volunteering at a soup kitchen at St. Mary's Catholic Church in Bloomington, Illinois. Taking a break, McHale sat in his car and listened to the National Public Radio affiliate WGLT, broadcast from the Illinois State University campus. The station featured breaking news that U.S. Attorney Patrick Fitzgerald had issued an indictment of Governor Rod Blagojevich on a number of counts of corruption. McHale immediately called Seay, and the two discussed how this was the third act for which Seay sought.

In the weeks following Blagojevich's arrest, the state legislature in Springfield scrambled to start the process of kicking the governor out of office. During one instance specifically, Seay had responsibilities as a teaching graduate instructor which overlapped with a hearing in Springfield. He called McHale and inquired about whether he should suspend his responsibilities in order to cover impeachment proceedings against Rod Blagojevich. McHale encouraged Seay to gather footage of the unfolding drama at the expense of Seay's other responsibilities. Thus, it was an indicative example that the documentarian must gather footage of events as they unfold. In the case of a documentary, gathering footage of key events may only come once, and the effective documentarian is wise to place an extremely high priority on taking advantage of opportunities to gather such footage.

Scripting documentary is a more recursive process than writing many other types of scripts, such as television programs or dramatic films, because documentaries usually are restricted to what actually happened as captured on videotape or film rather than what can be dramatically created or re-created. In televisual production, a script usually is completed and shooting schedules are generated based on the shots in the script. In documentary production, however, the initial script is a shot "wish list," and footage is gathered with the understanding that additional footage might be needed as the shots on the wish list are whittled down. Simply put, the makers of documentary cannot plan on gathering footage that is exactly what they want; they must work with the footage they get. As Walters (1994) suggested, "In the true documentary, in contrast to programs that are re-creations, the sequences cannot be scripted in detail in advance; they can only be loosely planned" (p. 449). Footage of what actually happened is logged as the best selections are noted.

Revising the Plan in Editing

Editing is the central aspect of post-production. One of the communicative powers of video, as with film, is its ability to juxtapose images and sound, with the arrangement of the shots creating a cumulative meaning and effect that transcends the individual images and sounds. Technology also has made the editing process easier; advances in editing and special effects software enabled Seay to craft the finished product. Seay, as the editor, did most of the actual arrangement of video clips into a unified whole in accordance with the plans he had developed in the script. Seay was also responsible for generation of the graphics and other effects that were used in the video documentary, such as super-imposition of multiple shots in one frame and all computer-generated fonts.

Sometimes, the written plan does not play out effectively on screen. Perhaps some footage couldn't be captured or an event didn't happen the way it was previously thought to happen. As mentioned, the script is always evolving. But once the documentary crew's efforts reach the editing room, practical decisions must be made about how to effectively communicate the drama on screen. This is the most important time of the script evolution, because what happens here will ultimately be seen by the audience.

Seay also had a variety of *b-roll shots* (video shots, also called *inserts* or *cut-aways*, that can be used under the voice-over provided by an anchor or a reporter to increase the visual variety within the story) written into the script that had to be shot. These b-roll shots included locations, maps, and other visual elements referred to in the documentary. In the editing process, we would cut to these shots to visually reinforce the words being spoken, as well as to provide some variety, for Seay did not want the documentary to simply be a series of talking heads. There has been some controversy over the inclusion of dramatic re-creation in documentary (see, e.g., Walters, 1994). The rise of *cinema verite* (the emphasis in video/film on actuality and on the role of the makers of a documentary in the situation rather than their *representation* of reality) has lessened the use of director reconstruction of what may have happened (Bruzzi, 2000).

Promotion and Exhibition

Seay also had challenges after he actually finished the video documentary in terms of showing it at as many venues as possible and promoting all of the events that accompanied its exhibition. The final documentary, *Pontiac's Rebellion,* was initially screened at a high school in Pontiac. This provided an opportunity for advocates and other community members to celebrate their successful campaign and the resulting decision by the new governor, Patrick Quinn, to keep the Pontiac Correctional Center open and operational. The documentary also was featured at two regional video/film festivals as well as a stand-alone showing at Illinois State University and a screening at the ISU Documentary Project Socio-political Film Festival, where Seay also received the 2010 Voice of Conscience Award. The festivals provided the opportunity to educate more people in Illinois on the case of the Pontiac Correctional Center and the potential for motivated individuals to make a difference in their community through political involvement and activity.

This qualitative research involved the search for emic knowledge (an understanding of events from the perspective of those who live them) as opposed to etic knowledge (knowledge gathered from an outsider observing a scene) (Lindlof & Taylor, 2002). Thus, ethnographic methods of data collection and qualitative analysis of those data (using the process of constant comparison) guided is summary of the process of writing and producing a documentary on a local political issue campaign.

Lessons Learned About Communication Activism

This chapter has described an example of the writing and production of a documentary on a local political campaign to oppose a decision of questionable value by Governor Blagojevich. There are several lessons about communication activism that can be learned from this experience.

First, the presence of someone working on a documentary as activist fight for their cause may increase the morale of the activist. The production of a documentary may help persuade people to take note and become involved in a local issue campaign.

Second, scholars need to take advantage of available resources for engaging in communication activism. University environments can provide much support to scholars who seek to make a positive difference in their communities. In general, ISU was supportive of Seay's efforts. Overall, the university environment in which Seay worked was supportive of our effort and appreciated the publicity generated from the project. Activist scholars, thus, should take advantage of available resources and try to generate positive media coverage for the university in which they work.

Third, this project demonstrated that the theory of advocacy communication (McHale, 2004) and similar scholarship can inform an advocacy campaign (see, e.g.,

Goodman, 2003; Nichols, 1981, 1991, 1994; Ryan, 1991; Ryan et al., 1998), and this interaction between communication scholarship and activism offers many lessons for scholar-activists. The recursive nature of this research and video production can be useful for others seeking to study activism at the same time that they assist activist efforts. Lessons were learned about the production and distribution of a video documentary, sharing information, coordinating activists' efforts, working with representatives from news outlets, and organizing lobbying efforts. The lesson here is that *praxis* (the combination of theory, research, and practice) is an effective way to write and produce a documentary on a local issue-oriented political campaign.

Another valuable lesson from this work supports Whiteman's (2004) contention that scholarship needs to emphasize the possibilities for video/film documentaries to have broad social influence rather than considering such effects solely within an individualistic framework (e.g., effects on individuals' beliefs, attitudes, and values). For instance, the impact of documentaries must be considered as one of a number of factors that can influence governmental action. The mere presence of documentarians offered a legitimizing influence on the local political advocates. Unfortunately, past research has neglected the study of the process of writing and producing a documentary on a political issue in a local community. We have tried to address these issues in this research, and the result is a more organic picture of how video/film documentary on a political issue can be written and produced.

One of the most important lessons from this experience is that the production and exhibition of a video/film documentary can be useful in the fight for social justice if there are links made between the documentary and the larger political campaign. In this instance, there were extensive links between our work on the documentary and the fight to keep Pontiac Correctional Center open.

Finally, every project has elements that could have gone better and much can be learned from these instances. We hope this chapter can help future documentarians in their efforts to document issue-oriented political campaigns.

Conclusion

The story of the production of *Pontiac's Rebellion*, as in all cases of documenting activism, is one of *gumption*, a word of old Scottish origin that refers to activists' will to advocate and their enthusiastic enactment of advocacy communicative *praxis*—action in the public realm or *polis* informed by theory and research. Seay was fueled by the injustice of the impending closing of the prison in Pontiac and his belief that his documentary could effectively communicate about the closing of the facility. Gumption, thus, drove the production of *Pontiac's Rebellion*, as is necessary in making documentaries on all advocacy efforts. Seay's experiences, thus, show that video/film production is an important form of communication activism that can assist people in marginalized groups to secure political justice.

In this chapter, we identified the evolution of the story as seen through the development of *Pontiac's Rebellion* (2009). This case study provided an indicative example of how writing a documentary is a cyclical process, during which writers may develop an initial plan, but will be subject to changing nature of the real-life drama unfolding before them. We focused on that evolution through initial concept formulation, writing the treatment, constructing a shot wish list, amending the plan while shooting, and revising the story in editing. Again, to be successful, the documentary writer must "go with the flow."

Neal: How am I supposed to go with the flow when the rental car agency leaves me in a 100 acre parking lot with keys to a car that isn't there then I have to hike back 3 miles to find out they don't have any more cars?

Del: I got a car, no sweat at all.

Neal: Well Del, you're a charmed man.

Del: Nope.

Neal: Oh, I know. You just go with the flow.

Del: Like a twig on the shoulders of a mighty stream.

—*Planes, Trains, and Automobiles* (1987)

References

Adorno, T. (1991). *The culture industry: Selected essays on mass culture.* New York: Routledge.

Allen, M. (1998). Comparing the persuasive effectiveness one- and two-sided message. In M. Allen & R. W. Preiss (Eds.), *Persuasion: Advances through meta-analysis* (pp. 87-98) Cresskill, NJ: Hampton Press.

Bandura, A. (1971). *Psychological modeling: Conflicting theories.* Chicago: Aldine-Atherton.

Barnouw, E. (1993). *Documentary: A history of the non-fiction film* (2nd rev. ed.). New York: Oxford University Press.

Benoit, P. J. (1997). *Telling the success story: Acclaiming and disclaiming discourse.* Albany: State University of New York Press.

Bohn, T. (1977). *An historical and descriptive analysis of the "Why we fight" series: With a new introduction.* New York: Arno Press.

Bruzzi, S. (2000). *New documentary: A critical introduction.* New York: Routledge.

Durkheim, E. (1933 [1902]). *The division of labor in society.* (G. Simpson, Trans). Glencoe, IL: Free Press.

Fairhurst, G. T. (1993). The leader-member exchange patterns of women leaders in industry: A discourse analysis. *Communication Monographs, 60,* 321-351.

Feldman, S., & Sigelman, L. (1985). The political impact of prime-time television: "The Day After." *Journal of Politics, 47,* 557-578.

Fiske, J., & Hartley, J. (1978). *Reading television.* London: Methuen.

Fromm, E. (1976). *To have or to be?* New York: Harper & Row.

Gerbner, G. (1999). Cultivation analysis: An overview. *Mass Communication & Society, 3-4,* 175-194.

Glaser, B. G., & Strauss, A. L. (1967). *The discovery of grounded theory: Strategies for qualitative research.* Chicago: Aldine.

Goodman, S. (2003). *Teaching youth media: A critical guide to literacy, video production and social change.* New York: Teachers College Press.

Hall, S. (1982). The rediscovery of "ideology": Return of the repressed in media studies. In M. Gurevitch, T. Bennett, J. Curran, & J. Woolacott (Eds.), *Culture, society and the media* (pp. 56-90). New York: Methuen.

Hart, R. D., & Williams, D. E. (1995). Able-bodied instructors and students with physical disabilities: A relationship handicapped by communication. *Communication Education, 44,* 140-154.

Hovland, C. I., Janis, I. L., & Kelly, H. H. (1953). *Communication and persuasion: Psychological studies of opinion change.* New Haven, CT: Yale University Press.

Hughes, J. (1987). *Planes, Trains, and Automobiles.*

Janis, I. L., Hovland, C. I., Field, P. B., Linton, H., Graham, E., Cohen, A. R. et al. (1959). *Personality and persuasibility.* New Haven, CT: Yale University Press.

Katz, E., & Lazarsfeld, P. F. (1955). *Personal influence: The part played by people in the flow of communications.* Glencoe, IL: Free Press.

Klapper, J. T. (1960). *The effects of mass communication.* Glencoe, IL: Free Press.

Lange, J. I. (1993). The logic of competing information campaigns: Conflict over old growth and the spotted owl. *Communication Monographs, 60,* 239-257.

Lasswell, H. D. (1935). *World politics and personal insecurity.* New York: Whittlesey House, McGraw-Hill.

Lenart, S., & McGraw, K. (1989). America watches "Amerika": Television docudrama and political attitudes. *Journal of Politics, 51,* 697-712.

Lindlof, T. R., & Taylor, B. C. (2002). *Qualitative communication research methods* (2nd ed.). Thousand Oaks, CA: Sage.

Lippmann, W. (1922). *Public opinion.* New York: Harcourt, Brace.

Lorentz, P. (1936). *The Plow that Broke the Plains.*

Lorentz, P. (1937). *The River.*

Marcuse, H. (1964). *One dimensional man: Studies in the ideology of advanced industrial society.* Boston: Beacon Press.

McCombs, M. E., & Shaw, D. L. (1972). The agenda-setting function of mass media. *Public Opinion Quarterly, 36,* 176-187.

McHale, J. P. (2004). *Communicating for change: Strategies of social and political advocates.* Lanham, MD: Rowman & Littlefield.

McHale, J. P. (2007). Using documentary to promote justice. In L. Frey & K. Carragee (Eds.), *Communication Activism.* Cresskill, NJ: Hampton Press.

McHale, J. P. (Producer/Director), Wylie, R. (Producer/Editor), & Huck, D. (Producer/Assistant Editor). (2002). *Unreasonable doubt: The Joe Amrine case* [Videotape].

Moore, M. (1989). *Roger and Me.*

Moore, M. (2002). *Bowling for Columbine.*

Moore, M. (2004). *Fahrenheit 9/11.*

Morris, E. (1988). *Thin Blue Line.*

Morris, E. (2003). *Fog of War.*

Nichols, B. (1981). *Ideology and the image: Social representation in the cinema and other media.* Bloomington: University of Indiana Press.

Nichols, B. (1991). *Representing reality: Issues and concepts in documentary.* Bloomington: Indiana University Press.

Nichols, B. (1994). *Blurred boundaries: Questions of meaning in contemporary culture.* Bloomington: Indiana University Press.

Noelle-Neumann, E. (1984). *The spiral of silence: Public opinion, our social skin.* Chicago: University of Chicago Press.

Peterson, T. R., Witte, K., Enkerlin-Hoeflich, E., Espericueta, L., Flora, J. T., Florey, N., Loughran, T., & Stuart, R. (1994). Using informant directed interviews to discover risk orientation: How formative evaluations based in interpretive analysis can improve persuasive safety campaigns. *Journal of Applied Communication Research, 22,* 199-215.

Reeves, N. (1999). *The power of film propaganda: Myth or reality?* New York: Cassell.

Riefenstahl, L. (1934). *Triumph of the Will.*

Ryan, C. (1991). *Prime time activism: Media strategies for grassroots organizing.* Boston: South End Press.

Ryan, C., Carragee, K. M., & Schwerner, C. (1998). Media, movements, and the quest for social justice. *Journal of Applied Communication Research, 26,* 165-181.

Sabourin, T. C., & Stamp, G. H. (1995). Communication and the experience of dialectical tensions in family life: An examination of abusive and nonabusive families. *Communication Monographs, 62,* 213-242.

Schramm, W. (1954). *The process and effects of mass communication.* Urbana: University of Illinois Press.

Schramm, W., Lyle, J., & Parker, E. B. (1961). *Television in the lives of our children.* Stanford, CA: Stanford University Press.

Seay, B. (2009). *Pontiac's Rebellion.*

Stamp, G. H. (1994). The appropriation of the parental role through communication during the transition to parenthood. *Communication Monographs, 61,* 89-112.

Strauss, A., & Corbin, J. (1998). Basics of qualitative research: Techniques and procedures for developing grounded theory (Rev. ed.). Thousand Oaks, CA: Sage.

Tönnies, F. (1940 [1887]). *Fundamental concepts of sociology (Gemeinschaft und gesellschaft).* (C. P. Loomis, Trans). New York: American Book.

Tracy, K., & Baratz, S. (1993). Intellectual discussion in the academy as situated discourse. *Communication Monographs, 60*, 300-320.

Walters, R. L. (1994). *Broadcast writing: Principles and practices* (2nd ed.). New York: McGraw-Hill.

Whiteman, D. (2004). Out of the theaters and into the streets: A coalition model of the political impact of documentary film and video. *Political Communication, 21*, 51-69.

Youngs, J. (2003, September 19). Amrine, activists speak out at rally. *The Maneater*, p. 1.

Zarefsky, D. (1980). A skeptical view of movement studies. *Central States Speech Journal, 31*, 245-254.

Zemans, F. K. (1983). Legal mobilization: The neglected role of the law in the political system. *American Political Science Review, 77*, 690-703.

Zillman, D., & Weaver, J. B. (1997). Psychoticism in the effects of prolonged exposure to gratuitous media violence on the acceptance of violence as a preferred means of conflict resolution. *Personality and Individual Difference, 22*, 613-627.

Chapter 10

Writing a Film Treatment:

Tips from a Hollywood Insider

by

Alex Hedlund

There is an urban legend in Hollywood about a no-name screenwriter who got his big break after pitching Steven Spielberg during a chance encounter in an elevator. Regardless of the validity of such a story, your best bet for selling your movie idea is not by stalking elevators but through a written outline called a "treatment." This essay establishes the basics of treatment writing so that any novice can learn to tell a visual story like a Hollywood professional. Through this essay, you should be able to identify the main purpose of writing a film treatment, learn the proper treatment format, and ascertain a few strategies used by professional writers.

The goal of any treatment is twofold: thoroughly, but succinctly synopsize your movie and hook the reader, which could be a producer, studio head, or agent. You may have no experience pitching a big Hollywood producer, but you have probably recommended a movie to someone by saying, "It's about someone who..." A treatment is the same idea, only in the form of a written document for potential buyers. Treatments are not book reports. They are more akin to a written movie trailer. The majority of trailers run between one and two minutes in length and exist to sell the movie to the audience. While your treatment should contain more detail than a trailer, the final document should not surpass five pages. Anything beyond a few pages is asking too much of your reader. James Cameron is notorious for writing long documents called "scriptments" (*Avatar* exceeded 70 pages), but he is *the* James Cameron, winner of three Academy Awards and director of the two highest-grossing films of all-time, *Titanic* and *Avatar*.

Begin your treatment with a title and a "logline." The logline is a one-sentence synopsis of your idea that details your character(s), central conflict, goal, and stakes. Your treatment will expand on these ideas at length, but it is crucial to grab the reader's attention first. If you cannot successfully synthesize your idea into one sentence, the chances of finding a movie-executive willing to finish the rest of your treatment are low. Think of it like reading a *TV Guide* entry: *Seven* is about two detectives, a veteran and a rookie, tracking a serial killer who kills according to the seven deadly sins. *Gladiator* follows an imprisoned Roman general who fights as a gladiator in the hope of avenging his murdered family. The more defined your movie idea, the easier it is to boil it down into one sentence. If you have problems paring down your thoughts, you may have serious story issues to address.

Another useful strategy to employ when writing a logline is to provide a comparison film or "comp." Comps are similar films that help establish tone, subject matter, or scale in your reader's mind. For example, using a comp like *The Hangover* rather than *Liar Liar* can help clarify that you are pitching an edgy, R-rated laugher rather than a general comedy for a broader audience. Marketing execs often use the same method in trailers. Lines such as "From the director/producers of..." often evoke familiar titles in the hopes of attracting a similar audience. Use that same theory in your treatment by opening with, "A horror film in the vein of *The Exorcist* about (logline)" or "An inspiring true story like *The Blind Side* about (logline)." Be careful though, as a bad comp could potentially turn off your reader and kill your project instantly. Always reference a hit or prestige film in your comparison. Never use box office flops or obscure films your reader may not have seen as a comp. If your movie is a big budget action-adventure, a comp such as *Waterworld* is not an encouraging sales tool. While the scale and scope may be similar, *Waterworld* is a well-documented bomb, and you do not want that kind of negative comparison with your idea. Instead, consider comps such as *Raiders of the Lost Ark* or *Pirates of the Caribbean*.

Additionally, avoid the urge to use multiple comps or the clichéd "this meets that" pitch (e.g., *Star Wars* meets *Titanic*.) While the "meets" formula is often seen in marketing campaigns, there is potential to confuse and alienate the viewer. Trying to crossbreed two successful films, which may each have potent elements comparable to your own project, can often backfire because those comps are very polarizing. In short, pick one comp and stick with it.

When introducing a character for the first time, list their name in all capital letters (FORREST GUMP) and include a brief description to visualize the character. It is important to impart each character with a defining characteristic, personality trait, or profession to make them more memorable. Give these characters genuine reasons for existing in the story, especially your leads. Is your hero sympathetic and motivated? Do we want them to succeed? Do they go through any emotional or physical change during the course of the story? Always show, don't tell. Do not simply explain "this is my hero and this is my villain." Provide visual cues which demonstrate why we should root for this hero and why this villain is the very epitome of evil.

Additionally, discuss the major conflict in the film. Without crisis or obstacles in every scene, you risk disengaging your audience. The story drags and characters begin to feel lethargic. There must be a clear sense of conflict that serves as catalytic for your main character(s) and establishes numerous obstacles to overcome throughout the course of the film. *Die Hard* is a classic action film because it pits John McClain as a lone cop against an entire group of terrorists in an office building. We like McClain because he is a quintessential everyman, and, perhaps more importantly, he succeeds despite great odds. If McClain had an entire police force at his disposal, the movie would end immediately, and the resolution would lack excitement. Conversely, the stakes do not always need to be life and death. While primal concerns feel most appropriate in action and horror films, the stakes can be much lower depending on the tone and subject matter. In *Little Miss Sunshine*, the stakes involve a family's cross-country trip to a beauty pageant, or your characters might strive to lose their virginity on prom night, as in *American Pie*. Define the stakes of the story early to establish expectations and guidelines for your characters.

In terms of story, you want to describe the beginning, middle, and end without going into too much detail. This treatment should be a comprehensive synopsis, but not the entire script. Avoid describing every individual scene. Focus in on the beats that keep the story moving to engage the reader. A movie like *The Departed* has many different storylines, and it is easy to trip over the cat-and-mouse dynamics and motivations of all the characters. Stress concision whenever possible and adhere to the actions of the main characters for reference. A side character such as "Thug #3" may have a few lines of dialogue in the script but does not merit mention in your treatment. Most importantly, always highlight the bigger moments typically referred to as "set pieces." Every movie, hopefully, has several set pieces. The troops' storming of Omaha Beach in the opening of *Saving Private Ryan* is a set piece. The awkward dinner scene in *Meet the Parents* is an example of a comedic set piece. Even smaller, dialogue-heavy films such as *The Social Network* and *Moneyball* contain set pieces.

One common mistake when pitching any idea is telling your audience how to react to the material rather than eliciting the intended emotions organically from your story. Telling someone, "This is the funniest idea you'll ever hear," is a table setting for disappointment because comedy is subjective. Such a statement passes judgment on your audience. Do not ramble off the logline and explain that the film is funny—*show* them why they should laugh, or better yet, actually make them laugh! If you pitch a comedy, describe a few scenes and the sources of humor (sight gags, dialogue, bathroom humor, etc.). The same rule applies for every genre; if you pitch an action film, write about car chases, explosions, or gun fights. When pitching a horror movie, discuss big scares, monsters, or creepy ambiance. Try to visualize those great trailer moments that help sell the promise of the premise and dictate those into your treatment.

In summary, always remember the two primary goals of writing a film treatment: be as concise as possible when outlining your movie while hooking the reader with dramatic elements and visual cues. Using proper treatment format, such as having a succinct logline and limiting the number of pages of your treatment, builds credibility with your audience. Employing treatment strategies, such as using favorable comps and evoking emotion without telling your audience explicitly how to react, help to generate imagery in the mind of your reader. Following these guidelines can both improve your writing skills and bolster your treatment as a potential calling card for breaking into Hollywood. At the very least, you can prepare for your own big break, should Steven Spielberg step into that next elevator.

Edited by Mike Firmand

About Alex Hedlund

Alex Hedlund, originally from Urbana, Illinois, has over four years of behind-the-scenes experience in Hollywood. He received two degrees from the University of Illinois, a B.S. in Media Studies in 2005 and a M.S. in Journalism in 2006. After earning a MFA in the Producers Program at UCLA in 2008, Alex worked under creative executives at Warner Bros. Pictures and Stars Road Entertainment. Alex currently operates as a Creative Executive at Legendary Entertainment tracking potential projects in the form of movie and television scripts, comic books, video games, and other intellectual property.

Chapter 11

Old Radio Ideas in New Media Style

by

Zach Parcell

The radio industry is changing. Day by day, it is evolving from a narrowly focused medium to a full-blown, multimedia phenomenon. Radio still has over-the-air programming—music, local talk, sporting events, the list goes on. But now, with the addition of online web streaming and mobile apps, the audience can always listen, even if they are out of range of the station's over-the-air signal.

The on-air product is not the only thing that has evolved. A radio station's website is quickly becoming one of its most important assets. In the past, radio station websites have been driven by promotions and sales, and supported by content. Now, they are becoming content driven and supported by promotions and sales. The on-air staffs of radio stations are adding the title of "Blogger" next to "Morning Show Host." For years, a DJ would go on the air and talk about the latest celebrity gossip, sports story, upcoming local event, or a new single from the most popular artist. Now, after talking about it on the air, they are turning their 30-second stopsets into multimedia blog posts.

Put yourself in the shoes of a broadcaster. You host an afternoon drive show on a Top 40 (Contemporary Hit Radio). Your on-air shift starts at two o'clock and ends at seven. You also need to write two blog posts a day. These blog posts are an extension of your show.

What do I write about?

The most common problem, when writing a blog post, is coming up with something to write about. An easy way to start is to think of five things that interest you. They can be specific or very broad: sports, the Chicago Bears, cooking, grilling, rock music, the local music scene, hunting and fishing, movies, standup comedy, running, etc. These are the things that you do on a daily or weekly basis. What do you love to do on your free time? What are you passionate about? Help share your passion for things like this and write them up in a few posts.

Then think of five things that your audience is interested in, things like local events, celebrity news, the funny video everyone is talking about at work, or winning prizes.

Look! You now have 10 topics. Start with that. If a radio station has five people on staff, and if you allow for some overlap, you could have easily 35 to 50 topics that will show up on your website. Those topics will pull in a great audience.

Go beyond the obvious. For example, what would you expect to find on a rock station's website/blog? You might see news about rock music, "babe of the day" content (sex sells), or sports. Why not write about the Hollywood gossip but with a sarcastic tone? What about food? Give local reviews of the best burgers in town. Why not find the best bars for sporting events? Or the best live music?

If you talked about it on the air, it should be on your website. Don't tell listeners that this funny video is on YouTube. Tell them that it is the latest post on your website. Make it easier for the listener to find it. You can also create features that show up on the blog on a regular basis.

Ok, I have what I want to write about. How long should my post be?

The length of a blog can be a tricky thing to nail down. Remember that you're writing for a blog, not a magazine or a newspaper. These posts do not need to be more than a few paragraphs to be effective. Could you write a very effective post in just a paragraph or two? Of course you can. Could you also write one that is a couple thousand words long? Sure, but make sure it is what your audience wants. If it is a fun, lighthearted post then don't draw it out longer than it needs to be.

Think of a blog post in three parts. First, why did you want to write this post? Is the content funny? A "must read" for your audience? What makes it intriguing? Make the reader read beyond the first paragraph. This is your hook. If someone read just the first paragraph, would they continue to read it? Take out any photos, too. Just consider the text. Your first paragraph needs to be juicy. A juicy paragraph is something that gives readers an idea of what the story is about but doesn't answer every question they have. It forces them to continue to read the post and stay on your site.

The second part is the meat of your post. Give readers the details. Show the video. Embed the audio. This is why they came to your post.

For the third part, consider why your audience cares about this post. Is there a local angle? What happens next? What could this mean? What does your audience think? Ask that question and field comments. Not all of these questions are appropriate for every post, but this is where you can wrap up a nice post. A post with an ending that brings in the audience will continue to have life. What started as a post can turn into a conversation with readers. Be sure to keep an eye on comments. This can lead to a great follow-up post as well.

Do I need to follow AP style or another format? How formal should I be?

When it comes to writing style, don't stress. A blog post is conversational. You can use contractions, and you could even use a little slang where appropriate. If you use certain slang, words, or phrases on the air, there is nothing wrong with putting them on the blog, too. Take how you would normally talk and put it into written form, to make it easy to read and easy to write. Of course, you can't forget about grammar and basic rules of writing, too.

Where can I find content?

One of the best things about writing in a blog style is that you can be flexible. Take a look at your favorite websites/blogs. You'll see at the end of many posts a source link. Sometimes these are very clear "Source: CNN." Those words would link to a story on CNN. You might also see it in brackets [CNN] or something similar.

Let's say Brad Pitt just donated $1 million to a school in California. It is quite the popular story and you want to put a story on your website about it. You weren't there, so you can't write a story without giving the source of your information. Without a source, it is plagiarism. Don't even attempt it. There is nothing wrong with using a

CNN.com story, TMZ.com story, or any other site that IS credible and who was there for this story. All you need to do is credit your story. For example:

If you're a high school principal you dream of the day when someone walks in with $1,000,000 to donate to your school. Luckily, for one Santa Clara High School, with some help from Brad Pitt, that dream came true. The Hollywood A-Lister donated the chunk of change earlier today to help support their theater department. [CNN]

[CNN] ← this is my source. I'd link "CNN" to the story on CNN.com. You could also link the words "donated the chunk of change earlier today" to that same story. This shows what your source is.

Always, always, always give credit for where you got your info. A post can easily look like you did all the leg work when in reality, you're taking info and putting your own spin/voice on it. If you just copy and paste or slightly rework a post, it looks fishy. Show some creativity. This is where you can have some fun with it. Put things in your own words and cite your source for the main points.

It also doesn't hurt to write in first person. If you loved some video, or you are talking about an event you attended, writing in first person allows the audience to connect with you.

Social media

Don't forget to share your post through social media. This is where your audience spends most of its day. People sit on sites like Facebook, Twitter, Tumblr, and Google Plus all day long. Realize that they don't spend all day on your radio station website (yet). Go to where your audience is and share your links. Start a conversation.

If you are getting comments and questions on Facebook about your post, don't forget to respond. Social media is more than just talking. It is also listening. If people are asking questions, give answers. If they have comments, build on top of those comments. You're working in radio. You might forget, but to many people, you're the fun radio personality. If you start a conversation with them, they'll feel excited about that. They'll keep coming back to your site and seeing your posts.

There is no such thing as the "perfect time" to post on Facebook. Some say it is the afternoon, some say the evening but there is no magic time of the day to post. No matter when you post, the most important thing is what you are sharing. Content is king. Content trumps everything. If you write a great post that your readers care about, your readers will share it with their friends.

The Cycle

You're on the air. There is an audience that tunes in every day. You wrote a blog post and talked about it on the air. That audience will view that post online and share it on their Facebook page. That blog post reaches a new audience; they might share the post themselves. While they are on your site, they see that you're giving away concert tickets in a few hours. They tune in to your show. Then the cycle starts all over again.

As we said at the start, radio is evolving. If you are an afternoon DJ, your shift may end at six o'clock, but your show never actually ends. You can get people talking about a blog post before you go on the air and continue that conversation during your show. Keep up with what your audience is saying on Facebook that evening.

Finally, there are two golden rules to remember: 1) content is king, and 2) have fun. If you keep both of those things in mind all the time, blogging will become second nature to you.

Edited by Jim Gee

About Zach Parcell

Zach Parcell is a 2008 graduate of Illinois State University with a B.S. in Mass Communication. While at Illinois State, Zach was an active member at the student radio station WZND. He held the positions of News Director, Sports Director, and News & Sports Operations Director. Zach spent 3.5 years at Radio Bloomington (WJBC, WBNQ, WBWN, WJEZ) in Bloomington, Illinois. He most recently held the position of Digital Program Director and was in charge of all website content for four radio station websites. He is currently working in the Public and Community Relations Department at Wolfram|Alpha in Champaign, Illinois. He maintains three company blogs and social media for the company.

Chapter 12

Writing for Social Media

by

Kristi Zimmerman

The rise of social media has drastically changed the way people communicate and share information. Not only are geographical limitations nonexistent with this new method of connectivity, but so too are the traditional means of spreading news to the masses.

Social media has instantaneously flipped the power balance between the media and the masses: rather than the media driving the message, the masses determine what stories or products are most newsworthy. People now have the ability to tell the media what they want to learn, purchase, share, and experience. Most importantly, the masses now hold the power to scrutinize, rate, and debunk—a terrifying new reality for advertisers and mass media distributers who, in the past, were not at the whim of internet review sites like Yelp.com, Glassdoor.com, and Zagat.com.

This fluctuation in power significantly alters the way advertisers and other mass media professionals communicate with their audiences. In addition to the standard *active* approach to communication, advertisers must now focus on being *reactive*.

Social media in itself is not a communication strategy. Rather, social media is a conduit: it provides a means for distributing information and connecting with an audience. When the Alexander Graham Bell invented the telephone, organizations did not rise up discussing their "telephone" strategy. Instead, they discussed how they could use the telephone as a part of their marketing campaign strategy.

The social media boom has made it easier to segment and reach target audiences, but with this new level of audience accessibility comes the need for new communication strategies. To effectively utilize this new channel of communication, professionals must determine their objective, identify and segment audiences into niche groups, craft a wide range of messages that appeal to the needs and expectations of each group, and, once the attention has been gathered, drive the audience with a specific call of action.

Audience

With the improvement of web analytics and other internet sourcing tools, the ability to reach a targeted audience via social media has never been easier. Platforms like Facebook and Twitter have the ability to track specific keywords located in a user's profile via their personal information, pages "liked" and daily activity, then enable advertisers to utilize this information in their communication strategies for a small fee.

Additionally, many of the major social networking platforms allow administrators to select a target audience out of their pool of followers for every message and update. On Facebook, for example, once a small following is built organically (via referrals and word-of-mouth or buzz marketing), messages and other forms of media can be shared to specific audiences if it only applies to one geographical location.

Obviously these technological advancements provide a golden opportunity for mass media professionals. The ability to reach a niche audience is available with minimal effort, but it is important that new strategies are employed for successful delivery. This new ease of segmentation introduces the need to reevaluate, restructure, and tailor a wider set of messages to suit each niche audience.

As in any other mode of mass media communication, the audience must be keenly identified before crafting a message (or series of messages, depending on the campaign). Who will the message target and why? Most importantly, what should the audience do with the information? What is the call to action?

When tailoring specific messages for a campaign, it is imperative to speak to the audience by employing their terminology and jargon—or by using language that attracts the audience and encourages them to read more. Every communication must include information that is relative, pertinent, and appealing.

An example of this strategy in action could be easily employed with a Twitter account belonging to a character-driven organization or a tourist attraction, such as Medieval Times (the dinner and tournament show). Although the audience itself is not

94

necessarily knowledgeable in medieval lore, nor are they likely to speak in a medieval fashion, followers expect that Medieval Times would utilize such verbiage on Facebook or Twitter. This approach makes the updates fun to read and humorous, thus attracting more loyal followers and more shares with friends and family. The viral capability of such a strategy is endless.

To retain loyal followers and spark activity, messages must also be *reactive* by approaching the desires, needs, and expectations of the audience.

A detailed example might be a consulting company that needs to hire five new consultants with information technology degrees. The individuals must also be proficient in C++ programming *and* have a specialization in video game design. With this recruitment campaign it is very important to prove legitimacy and to pique interest since this particular audience is a competitive one to attract. Every message must be written using language specific to this very niche group of individuals, but it must also include information that *matters* to the audience. To achieve this, the consulting company needs to identify the information that the audience cares about. Is it salary? Benefits? Training? Developmental opportunities? Or, is the project itself potentially appealing to this select group? Once that information is gathered and the language has been identified, the messages can be developed and distributed via any of the social media platforms available.

Messaging Strategies

Authors of social media messages must constantly provide information that the audience craves and requires to continue reading and following. More importantly, social media messages must be tailored for audience interaction by including a call to action.

It is important to remember that social media is *social*. If a message does not welcome the feedback or participation of followers, it will fail.

Structural Considerations

Like traditional methods of mass communication, with every message publicly posted on a social media platform one must incorporate the four structural considerations. Although there are similarities between this new communication medium and the more traditional forms, there are a few significant differences that must be recognized with each message.

1. **Unity**

    All messages must follow a unified tone that carries through with all modes of communication. Unlike traditional communication strategies, quality social media messaging carries a personal and down-to-earth element (which is ideally what makes it "social"). Therefore, communications must have a clearly defined persona or author—someone the audience feels like they know.

    On Facebook and Twitter, the audience wants to hear from a person rather than an organization. This tone will resonate with readers as it becomes familiar and, if applied well, will be eagerly expected.

2. **Pace**

    Social media communication typically requires more attention and upkeep when compared to traditional means of communication because it requires a constant flow of activity.

    It is important to update and post messages frequently, but at a pace that is appropriate (and may sometimes be defined by the audience). For example, if readers expect daily posts and updates from a Facebook page or Twitter account, that need must be fulfilled. If an audience requires multiple updates in a day or only a few a week, that must be determined as well. Regardless of the frequency, it is imperative that tone is consistent.

3. **Variety**

    Although consistency is key with pace and tone, variety in information is a vital part of social media messaging. Communications must be appealing to the audience and also provide relevant information that is helpful and worthy of attention.

    In mass media, information relevancy and worthiness change on a daily (if not hourly) basis. So too does the mood or vibe of messaging. To keep things spicy and interesting, messages should have a range of emotions from humorous to sad to monotone or matter-of-fact.

4. Climax

All messages must have value to pique interest and keep the audience coming back for more. An example might be a series of communications leading up to an announcement or an unveiling of information that is exciting and worthy to the audience. These series must be pertinent and must commit that the announcement will be revealed at a specific date or time.

Elements for Quality

There are four elements of mass media writing a writer needs to consider, to ensure quality social media communications:

1. Clarity

All messaging must have a clear purpose, a defined audience, and an apparent call to action. If a message is in response to an existing discussion, it must be relevant informative and appropriate for the audience. Responses must be done quickly and can also be informal to maintain that personal element that is so imperative in social media messaging, but that should never compromise clarity.

2. Concise

Facebook and Twitter updates include character limits that require an author to be concise.

When using Facebook it is important to avoid getting close to the character limitations, as readers lose interest with lengthy posts that require an extra click to read the full post.

Blogging is no exception. Extensive posts can be detrimental to the relevancy and credibility of a blog. There are millions of blogs updated on the internet every day that are competing for readers—that is, readers who have a very limited amount of time and a short attention span. The last thing they will read is a five-page essay about a breakfast sandwich.

The plethora of information posted every day on the internet can be incredibly daunting to the masses. For this reason it is imperative that authors "pack a punch" with every post by being concise, informational, pertinent, and entertaining. Language loaded with detail is off-putting and sometimes flat out annoying to an audience.

Attention spans are shrinking, but people still expect pizzazz. This can be a delicate balance to achieve and illustrates why social media messaging can be such a challenging beast to conquer.

3. Correct

Like any other form of mass media writing, social media messages must be factual and should never mislead. The only time a fallacy is acceptable in social media is if it corresponds to a satirical tone or a theme that is clearly known and understood by the audience.

4. Complete

All messaging must fulfill the needs of the audience and only be left open-ended when welcoming interaction and discussion. If left open to encourage interaction, the discussion must eventually have closure. For example, a writer could ask a question on a status update that requires clear answer. After leaving it open to the audience for a select amount of time, the answer must be provided as to not leave anything unknown. Typically the participants will be interested in knowing if their answer is right (and acknowledged for their apt response), so it is important to do so and to thank everyone for their insight and contribution.

Conclusion

The world of social media communication is vast and ever-changing. As this virtual world evolves and grows, so too will our understanding of how social media can be best used to reach our communication objectives. To continue to be effective on social media platforms, mass media professionals must be committed to this new communication channel—only with frequent use can new, valuable features be identified and utilized. Most importantly, dedication and persistency will help us gauge

the effectiveness of our strategy and allow us to determine what changes or additions must be made to successfully communicate in this space.

Edited by Jackson Pillow

About Kristi Zimmerman

Kristi Zimmerman is an internet marketing and social media consultant for a Fortune 1,000 organization in the insurance and financial services industry. Her professional passion is building a strong employment brand specifically focused for talent acquisition. She attended the University of Illinois in Urbana-Champaign for her undergraduate degree in Fine Arts and received her Master's Degree in Communication at Illinois State University in 2009. She currently resides in Chicago, Illinois. When she's not navigating the interwebs, she's either taking a Second City course in acting, running a local race, scoping out new Chicago hot-spots, or playing fetch with her cat, Bruce.

Chapter 13

Writing a Viral Video

by

Griffin Hammond

Before you set out to write a *viral video*—that is, a video that spreads quickly online, often earning millions of views on YouTube—you must recognize that videos aren't *born viral*; they *go viral*. It's more like a verb than an adjective. Viral videos *happen*. You can't—like too many PR agencies I've collaborated with—simply tag a video #*viral*, or worse, title it that way: "[brand name] Viral Video!" In fact, while writing your video, I recommend striking the word *viral* from your vocabulary.

Each minute, 72 hours of video are uploaded to YouTube. Most videos languish online without ever reaching a significant audience. Meanwhile, *Gangnam Style*, the high-energy Korean pop song, earned over 1 billion views in the final five months of 2012—the first YouTube video to break that milestone. One billion plays means humans have collectively spent 5,000 years watching *Gangnam Style*—as long as the history of Korea. The much-disliked music video *Friday*, starring 14-year-old Rebecca Black, earned more views than any other video in 2011. In 2010, it was the auto-tuned *Bed Intruder Song*—"Hide ya kids; hide ya wife!" And in 2009, Susan Boyle singing *I Dreamed A Dream*.

Of all the videos vying for attention, why these? Kevin Allocca, Trends Manager at YouTube, suggests there are three reasons why videos go viral: tastemakers, community participation, and complete unexpectedness.

On January 8, 2010, Paul "Bear" Vasquez uploaded to YouTube his excited reaction to a "double rainbow." But it wasn't until talk show host Jimmy Kimmel shared the video five months later that *Double Rainbow* became an internet sensation. Likewise, Rebecca Black's *Friday* sat virtually unnoticed until comedian Daniel Tosh mentioned it. Many, if not most viral videos rely on these *tastemakers*, as Allocca calls them, to deliver the initial surge of viewership. A video only goes viral if those initial viewers are inspired to share it. Or remix it! That's *community participation*. Finally,

Allocca argues "only that which is truly unique and *unexpected* can stand out in the way that these things have."

To a large degree, serendipity determines whether a video is discovered and goes viral, but as a producer, there are several practices that improve your odds: developing an audience, writing a clear script, and including tastemakers in your distribution plan. I'll explain these in reverse order.

Tastemakers

In November 2011, when I worked for State Farm, our public relations team was challenged to lower the number of cooking fires that occur on Thanksgiving Day. We learned that actor William Shatner had twice nearly set himself or his home ablaze while deep frying a Thanksgiving turkey, so we hired him. My job: produce a video that demonstrates the fire risks of deep-fried turkey and inspires homeowners to protect themselves through safe cooking techniques. With only three weeks before Thanksgiving to produce and share the video, we couldn't rely on viewers to gradually discover it—we needed tastemakers to quickly deliver our message.

During the writing process, I focused on the media as our primary audience. While they probably wouldn't air the complete three-minute video, they'd likely gravitate towards soundbites or exciting visuals. So instead of the realistic, documentary-style approach I usually employed for the company, I distilled Shatner's tale into a sillier, quotable melodrama—starting with his want of "a moister, tastier turkey," and hitting all the notes of the dramatic model, finishing with a flame-filled climax and somber resolution.

After uploading to YouTube, we pitched the video directly to the media. The combination of William Shatner, fiery images, and a degree of unexpected ridiculousness from State Farm resonated with reporters fishing for pre-Thanksgiving stories. *AdWeek* called the video "epic." *TIME* labeled it "bizarre," and *The Today Show*'s Savannah Guthrie said, "I think that's an Oscar-winning performance right there." Matt Lauer called it, "a little over the top."

That *over-the-top*ness is precisely what appealed to news outlets, and earned the video over 500,000 YouTube views, over $10 million in publicity value from broadcast impressions, and caused State Farm's Thanksgiving-Day cooking-fire claims to drop 34 percent. I'm proud of the video, but if not for the power of tastemakers—every major news organization that shared the video—no significant audience would have seen it.

Not every video can achieve epic levels of viewership like *Gangnam Style*, but the *virality* of any video is relative. State Farm's Thanksgiving video didn't even break 1 million views, but it certainly achieved their goals, and a level of viewership uncharacteristic of an insurance company. In 2010, I uploaded a video of my cat climbing our Christmas tree. When several tastemakers—in this case, cat blogs—discovered it, the video jumped to 100,000 views—far more than I'd expected. This tastemaker intervention is often a surprise, but a smart public relations campaign should write this phenomenon into the plan, to increase the odds of going viral.

Writing a Good Video

While many viral videos aren't actually scripted—like *Double Rainbow*, which depicts a real, live moment—they often incorporate characteristics of good writing. Vasquez's emotional response to a double rainbow is a series of contradictions: It's a stark contrast from the reaction you or I would likely have. It's in conflict with our expectation of how a grown man should react, and it's funny, because it's so unlikely. This conflict between our expectations and what's presented—that's drama. *Friday* is a dramatic video, showcasing Rebecca Black's poor singing, in conflict with her starring role in an oddly catchy music video.

Humans are hard-wired to gravitate towards drama, and conflict is the essence of the dramatic model. Even the words or structure you choose can infuse conflict into your writing. Newspaper headlines often highlight the contradiction between opposing ideas: "Brooklyn Pilot Plummets 1,000 Feet, Survives." To surprise viewers or make them laugh, video producers must consider how dramatic conflict will play against the audience's expectations.

Zach King, a college student in Los Angeles, has made a career of regularly producing —and earning ad revenue from—viral videos. A talented visual effects artist, King likes to mash up popular internet memes, such as *cats* and *Star Wars*, into YouTube videos like *Jedi Kittens*, which has earned millions of views. By tapping into pop culture topics that his audience enjoys, he's able to generate conflict against their expectations.

And don't forget: Good writing is good writing—whether it's journalism or video production. Aside from emphasizing conflict through dramatic storytelling, a script that is clear and concise will attract an audience.

Developing an Audience

Far too many PR/marketing professionals believe a single viral video is the ticket to elevate a brand—from zero followers to internet sensation. Sure, it worked for Rebecca Black, but cases like hers are rare. Most success in social media doesn't happen overnight; it takes years of audience development. PSY, the Korean pop superstar, uploaded 17 videos to YouTube before striking gold with *Gangnam Style*. A viral video is lifted by the fans who share it, so you're best served by developing this community *before* aspiring for viral success. A viral video is like a rolling snowball: The bigger the initial audience, the greater potential for growth.

Professional YouTube creators owe much of their success to YouTube's subscription model: Creators ask viewers to click *subscribe*, which notifies them when new videos are uploaded. Zach King's *Jedi Kittens* has earned over 4 million views. By encouraging those viewers to subscribe, his sequel—*Jedi Kittens Strike Back*—has earned twice as many views. King has spent years building a reliable audience, which ensures better odds that his subsequent videos will spread.

Whatever the social media platform—Facebook, Twitter, YouTube, etc.—you never want to start from scratch when challenged to spread your brand's message. It's better to lay the groundwork in advance: Upload several videos, experiment with the platform, establish your role in the community, and build an audience *before* attempting to go viral.

Going Viral

It's February 2013, and tens of thousands of people on YouTube have uploaded dance videos set to a song called *Harlem Shake*. The viral trend has collectively earned

175 million views so far. This popularity is ironic, because the song is copyrighted—none of the video creators can monetize their videos; all ad revenue will go to Mad Decent, the record label behind *Harlem Shake*. This is so often the case: viral videos spawn from those without a business agenda. Kevin Allocca's causes for viral videos—tastemakers, community participation, and complete unexpectedness—are biased against those seeking to make money. The media loves an underdog; communities rally around their own kind. And we expect big brands to spread messages across the globe, but it's so much more exciting when regular people become internet celebrities.

So if you become a public relations professional, and your boss asks you to write a viral video, it'll be an uphill climb—with the internet community biased against your money-making agenda. Yes, Baauer (the *Harlem Shake* artist) is making money, but odds are against a fan-made viral meme also sweeping your brand to success. To break through the noise, you must focus on developing an audience first, writing a clear, dramatic script, and incorporating tastemakers into the plan. Then, viral might happen to you.

About Griffin Hammond

Griffin is a video producer at YouTube Next Lab, where he creates tutorials for low-budget filmmakers. While working as a social media strategist on State Farm's public relations team, Griffin wrote and directed a fire safety video starring William Shatner, which won the Silver Anvil Award from the Public Relations Society of America.